The Science Chef is an exploratory guide to cooking with a scientific twist! It allows children to fully immerse themselves in making practical recipes that directly relate to scientific concepts. These easy-to-follow recipes create a natural blend of food and science and will engage young scientists of all ages.

Annamarie Russo, Supervisor of K-5 STEAM Education

The Science Chef series exemplifies the authors' passion for teaching kids. What a wonderful way to inspire scientific exploration by putting young culinary enthusiasts to work in the kitchen! Now more than ever, these books are important tools for educating kids at school or at home.

Ellen Taylor, Manager, The Farm Cooking School

The Science Chef is not your average cook book. The authors' brilliant concepts combine life and academic skills with delicious recipes. Math, science and culinary arts make cooking a truly interactive and multidisciplinary experience that kids can take from the classroom to their own family kitchens.

Darleen Reveille, RN,
Robert Wood Johnson Foundation Community Health Leader

THE SCIENCE CHEF

JOAN D'AMICO, EdD

GARFIELD SCHOOL DISTRICT, GARFIELD, NEW JERSEY

KAREN EICH DRUMMOND, EdD, RDN, LDN

GWYNEDD MERCY UNIVERSITY, GWYNEDD VALLEY, PENNSYLVANIA

THE SCIENCE CHEF

100+
Fun Food
Experiments and
Recipes for Kids

SECOND EDITION

JB JOSSEY-BASS™
A Wiley Brand

Jossey-Bass
A Wiley Imprint
111 River St, Hoboken, NJ 07030
www.josseybass.com

Jossey-Bass books and products are available through most bookstores. To contact Jossey-Bass directly, call our Customer Care Department within the U.S. at 800–956–7739, outside the U.S. at +1 317 572 3986, or fax +1 317 572 4002.

Wiley also publishes its books in a variety of electronic formats and by print-on-demand. Some material included with standard print versions of this book may not be included in e-books or in print-on-demand. If this book refers to media such as a CD or DVD that is not included in the version you purchased, you may download this material at http://booksupport.wiley.com. For more information about Wiley products, visit www.wiley.com.

Library of Congress Cataloging-in-Publication Data

Names: D'Amico, Joan, 1957- author. | Drummond, Karen Eich, author. |
  Cash-Walsh, Tina, 1960- illustrator.
Title: The science chef : 100 fun food experiments and recipes for kids /
  Joan D'Amico, Ed.D., Karen Eich Drummond, Ed.D., RDN, LDN ;
  illustrations by Tina Cash-Walsh.
Description: Second edition. | Hoboken, NJ : Jossey-Bass, [2020] | Includes
  index.
Identifiers: LCCN 2020021958 (print) | LCCN 2020021959 (ebook) | ISBN
  9781119608301 (paperback) | ISBN 9781119608325 (adobe pdf) | ISBN
  9781119608332 (epub)
Subjects: LCSH: Food—Juvenile literature. | Cooking—Juvenile literature.
  | Science—Experiments—Juvenile literature.
Classification: LCC TX355 .D3 2020 (print) | LCC TX355 (ebook) | DDC
  641.3—dc23
LC record available at https://lccn.loc.gov/2020021958
LC ebook record available at https://lccn.loc.gov/2020021959

Cover Design: Wiley
Cover Images: Shoots of green beans © KPG_Payless/Shutterstock, Close-Up Of Popcorn Against Yellow Background © Melica/Shutterstock, Science beakers © Paul Tillinghast/Getty Images

Printed in the United States of America

SECOND EDITION
SKY10020525_081920

To Christi, Alexa, and Kyle. May all your dreams come true.

—Joan D'Amico

For Caitlin.

—Karen Eich Drummond

Contents

About This Book

Welcome to the updated second edition of *The Science Chef* designed to help you learn about science in new and tasty ways. Whenever you cook, you use the science of chemistry to mix and heat ingredients to make something new, like bread from flour, yeast, and water or popcorn from corn kernels and heat. You learn about biology when you investigate fruits, seeds, grains, herbs, spices, and other products from nature that we eat. And you learn the science of nutrition when you think about how the substances in foods you eat affect your body.

The first section, "Discovering Science in the Kitchen," covers the basics about science, cooking skills and equipment, food safety, and nutrition. *Read it carefully before you do any of the experiments or try any of the recipes*.

Part I, "Questions, Questions, Questions," explores answers to science questions such as "Why does popcorn pop?" and "How does bread rise?" Part II, "No More Boxes, Cans, or Jars: Do It Yourself," invites you to make foods from scratch or grow foods, instead of buying them ready made at the store, using science to explain the steps. For example, you can make your own spaghetti sauce, ice pops, and cookie mix.

Each chapter explores a different science topic by giving you an experiment or activity you can do right in your kitchen, followed by easy-to-make recipes that are based on the experiment. Altogether there are over 100 experiments and recipes for you to try. Each experiment and activity include a purpose statement, a list of the materials you will need, the steps to follow, questions for you to answer, and an explanation of what happened.

To answer the questions, first find a notebook with at least 20 pages. Design a notebook cover that says *Science Chef Notebook* and tape or paste it on the notebook cover. Each time you do an experiment, write down the chapter number and title at the top of a sheet of paper. Then write down the number of the first question along with your answer. Continue to answer all questions—there are usually about three or four questions.

After doing the experiment or activity, you can have some fun making one or more of the recipes. For example, learn what makes popcorn pop, then make some sensational snacks such as Trail Mix Popcorn, or grow some herbs to use in Garden Fresh Tomato Sauce.

Each recipe is rated according to how much cooking experience is required. The easiest recipes are noted as Beginner. Intermediate recipes require some cutting and cooking with heat. Advanced recipes require higher level cooking skills, but only a few recipes are marked as advanced.

Always be sure you have an adult to guide you when the experiment or recipe asks you to use the oven, stove, electrical appliances, or a knife.

All recipes also:

- list the time you need to make them and the number of servings each recipe makes.

- use easy-to-find ingredients and standard kitchen equipment.

- are kid-tested and kid-approved.

- emphasize wholesome and plant-based ingredients.

Each chapter has a video showing how to prepare one of that chapter's recipes. The videos are found at www.wiley.com/go/sciencechef.

At the end of the book you'll find a nutrient analysis of each recipe, glossary full of definitions, and index. So get your apron on, roll up your sleeves, wash your hands, and get ready to become a science chef. We hope you have as much fun learning, cooking, and eating as we did writing this book for you!

We would also like to thank our peer reviewers: Michelle Durham, who previously worked as a professor of criminal justice and currently teaches in Fort Lauderdale (Florida), and Laura Thomas, a teacher at Meridian School, an International Baccalaureate World School in Round Rock, Texas.

Joan D'Amico
Wayne, New Jersey

Karen Eich Drummond
Yardley, Pennsylvania

Discovering Science in the Kitchen

To learn about science, you don't have to go any further than your kitchen. **Food science** uses scientific principles, such as chemistry and biology, to explain how foods cook and also how foods are processed and preserved so everyone has access to safe, nutritious food. Experiments in this book are designed to illustrate key scientific principles in how foods are prepared, such as how flour thickens a soup or sauce, and also how foods are grown and produced, including how yogurt is made.

The experiments use the **scientific method**, a step-by-step process used to investigate questions. A scientist makes a **hypothesis** that predicts an answer to the question. The hypothesis is then tested by making observations that often include measurements. The results are analyzed and then summarized in a conclusion. For example, you know that baking powder makes bubbles when mixed in water due to a chemical reaction, but you are not sure if the temperature of the water affects how many bubbles are made. So you decide to test a hypothesis that baking powder makes more bubbles in hot water. By adding baking powder to hot water and to cold water, you can observe if there was a difference in the amount of bubbles produced.

A few chapters have an activity instead of an experiment. The activities include growing an herb plant, making your own mayonnaise and yogurt, and learning about crystals in ice and sugar. Each experiment and activity illustrate a variety of scientific principles.

To be a good scientist, all you need to do is start with a question. For example, at home tonight someone is putting dried pasta into a pot of boiling water to cook. Your question may be, "What happens when spaghetti is cooked in boiling water?" With good observation skills you will notice that before being boiled, spaghetti is dry and hard. Then after cooking, it is swelled up in size and is soft enough to eat. So while spaghetti is cooking in the boiling water, it is absorbing water that makes it swell in size and also tender enough to eat.

Preparation and Cooking Skills

Chefs need to master cutting and measuring skills and the basics of mixing and stovetop cooking. Here are the skills you will be practicing as you try the recipes in this book.

Cutting

Foods are cut before cooking so that they will look good and cook evenly. Place the food to be cut on a cutting board and use a knife that is a comfortable size for your hand. To hold the knife, place your hand on top of the handle and fit your fingers around the handle. The grip should be secure but relaxed. In your other hand, hold the item being cut. Keep your fingertips curled under to protect them from cuts. Never cut toward part of your body. (See the "Safety Rules!" section of this chapter for more on how to cut safely.)

Here are some commonly used cutting terms you'll need to know.

rslice   To cut into uniform slices.

dice   To cut into cubes of the same size.

chop   To cut into irregularly shaped pieces.

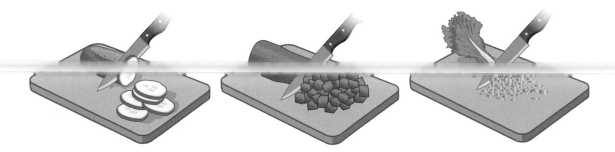

mince   To chop very fine into very small pieces.

grate   To rub a food across a grater's small punched holes, to produce small or fine pieces of food. Hard cheeses, such as parmesan, and some vegetables are grated.

Holes for grating hard cheese and other hard foods.

shred To rub a food across a surface with medium to large holes or slits. Shredded foods look like strips. The cheese used for making pizza is always shredded.

Shredding cheese

Measuring

Ingredients can be measured in three different ways: by counting (six apples), by measuring volume (½ cup of chopped apples), or by measuring weight (1 pound of apples).

To measure the volume of a liquid, use a measuring cup designed to measure liquids. Liquid measuring cups are usually made of glass and have a handle. Place the measuring cup on a flat surface and check that the liquid goes up to the proper line on the measuring cup while looking directly at it *at eye level*.

Measure liquids on a flat surface and look at eye level.

Measuring cups for dry ingredients such as flour are often made of metal. They are designed to be filled to the top and then leveled off. To measure the volume of a dry ingredient, such as flour, spoon it into the measuring cup and level it off with a table knife. Do not pack the cup with the dry ingredient—that is, don't press down on it to make room for more—unless the recipe says to. You can pack the cup when you are measuring brown sugar, butter, or margarine.

Level off dry ingredients with a table knife.

When cooking, you will most commonly work with cups, tablespoons, and teaspoons. One cup contains 16 tablespoons and one tablespoon contains 3 teaspoons.

3 teaspoons = 1 tablespoon

Following is a helpful measurement table.

Equivalents

1 tablespoon = 3 teaspoons

1 cup = 16 tablespoons

1 cup = 8 fluid ounces

1 quart = 2 pints

1 quart = 4 cups

1 quart = 32 fluid ounces

1 gallon = 4 quarts

1 stick butter or margarine = ½ cup = 8 tablespoons

Mixing

There are all kinds of ways to mix up ingredients! Here are definitions of the most common types.

mix	To combine ingredients so they are all evenly distributed.
beat	To move the utensil back and forth to blend ingredients together—same as mixing but a little more rigorous.
whip	To beat rapidly using a circular motion, usually with a whisk, to incorporate air into the mixture (such as in making whipped cream).
fold	To move the utensil with a gentle over-and-under motion.

| whisk | To beat ingredients together quickly with a wire whip. |
| cream | To mix a solid fat (usually butter) with sugar by pressing both against the bowl with the back of a spoon until they look creamy. |

Creaming butter and sugar to make cake or cookies.

Stovetop Cooking

There are different ways to cook on your stove. Here are descriptions of cooking methods you will be practicing as you try the recipes in this book. Because it is easy to get burned while cooking on the stove, see the "Safety Rules!" section of this chapter.

| boil | To heat a liquid to its boiling point, or to cook in a boiling liquid. Water boils at 212 °F (100 °C). You can tell it is boiling when you see lots of large bubbles popping to the surface. When a liquid boils, it is turning into steam (the gaseous state of water). Water can't get any hotter than 212 °F (100 °C); it can only make steam faster. Boiling is most often used for cooking pasta. |

simmer	To heat a liquid to just below its boiling point, or to cook in a simmering liquid. You can tell a liquid is simmering when it has some bubbles floating slowly to the surface. Most foods cooked in liquid are simmered. Always watch simmering food closely so you can turn down the heat if it starts to boil.
steam	To cook in steam. Steam has much more heat and cooks foods quicker than boiling water does. Steaming is an excellent method for cooking most vegetables.
sauté	To cook quickly in a pan over medium-high heat in a small amount of fat. Vegetables, such as onions, are often sautéed in oil to bring out their flavor and brown them.

Cracking and Separating Eggs

It is best to crack an egg into a clear glass cup or bowl before adding it to the other ingredients. That way if the egg smells bad or has a red spot, you can throw it out before the egg goes in with the other ingredients. An egg with a red spot is safe to eat but is usually thrown out because of its appearance. You should also check for eggshells in the egg before adding the egg to the other ingredients.

Sometimes you will need to separate the egg yolk from the egg white for a recipe. To do this, crack the egg over an egg separator and a bowl. Make sure you get the yolk in the middle. The holes in the bottom of the egg separator allow the whites to drain into the bowl.

An egg separator—whites drain into the bowl.

If you don't have an egg separator, you can separate an egg by cracking it over a bowl, keeping the yolk in one half of the shell. Carefully pass the egg yolk from one half of the shell to the other without letting it break until the whites have all fallen into the bowl.

Pots, Pans, and More!

Let's take a close look at the cooking equipment in your kitchen. These are the basic tools you'll need to do the experiments and prepare the recipes in this book. Any kitchen tools that are used in only one or two recipes are described within those recipes.

Pots and Pans

saucepan: (also called pot) Used for general stovetop cooking, such as boiling pasta or simmering a sauce.

Dutch oven: A large cooking pot with a lid. Excellent for stews, soups, and braising meat.

Saucepan

Dutch oven with lid

steamer basket: A perforated metal basket used to hold vegetables or other foods over steaming water in a saucepan.

Saucepan with steamer basket

frying pan: (also called a skillet) Used for cooking foods, such as hamburgers or onions, in fat or oil.

griddle: A flat surface without sides used for cooking pancakes, French toast, and bacon.

Baking Pans and Tools

baking pan: A square or rectangular pan used for baking and cooking foods in the oven. The most common sizes are 9 × 13 inch and 8-inch or 9-inch square.

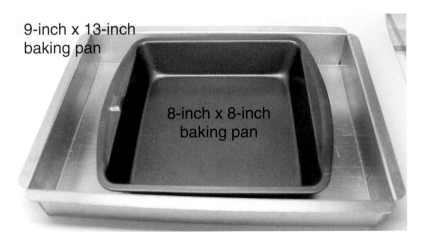

layer cake pans: Round metal pans used to bake layers of a cake.

loaf pan: A rectangular metal or glass pan with slanted walls. Used in both baking (for breads, for example) and cooking (such as for meat loaf).

Round cake pan

Loaf pan

cookie sheet: A large rectangular pan with no sides or with half-inch sides, used for baking cookies and other foods. May also be called *sheet pan* when it has sides.

Cookie sheets

muffin tins: Pans with small, round cups used for baking muffins and cupcakes.

Muffin pan

tube pan: A metal cake pan with a center tube used for making angel food cakes, sponge cakes, and special breads.

biscuit cutter: A round piece of metal used to cut biscuits from dough.

wire rack: Used for cooling baked goods.

rolling pin: A wooden or plastic roller used to flatten items such as pie crust and biscuit dough.

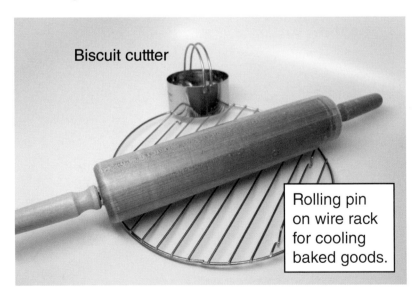

Biscuit cuttter

Rolling pin on wire rack for cooling baked goods.

Cutting Tools

cutting board: Made from wood or plastic, cutting boards provide a surface on which to cut foods.

paring knife: A knife with a small pointed blade used for trimming and paring vegetables and fruits and other cutting jobs that don't require a larger knife. (Most recipes in this book call for a knife, and a paring knife will work fine in most cases.)

peeler: A handheld tool that removes the peel from fruits and vegetables.

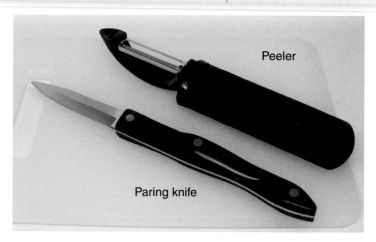

Peeler

Paring knife

sandwich spreader: A knife with a dull blade that is designed to spread fillings on bread.

grater: Used for shredding and grating foods such as vegetables and cheese.

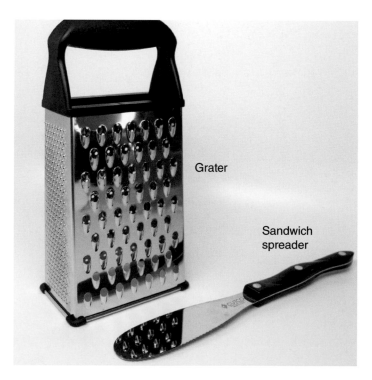

Grater

Sandwich spreader

Mixing Tools

blender: A glass or plastic cylinder with a rotating blade at the bottom used to make soups and smoothies. The blender has different speeds and handles liquids better than food processors.

food processor: A wide mixing bowl for ingredients and different attachments to slice, shred, and do other kitchen tasks.

Food processor

Blender

electric mixer: Two beaters that rotate to mix ingredients together. Used for mashed potatoes, cake batters, and other mixing jobs.

mixing bowls: Round-bottomed bowls used for mixing and whipping all kinds of foods.

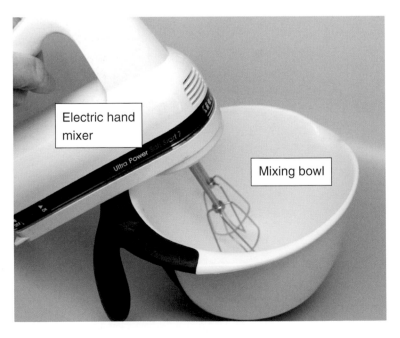

Electric hand mixer

Mixing bowl

wooden spoon: Used for mixing ingredients together and stirring.

wire whip (also called whisk): Used especially for whipping egg whites and cream.

rubber spatula: A flexible rubber or plastic tip on a long handle. It is used to scrape bowls, pots, and pans and for folding (a gentle over-and-under motion) ingredients into whipped cream or other whipped batter.

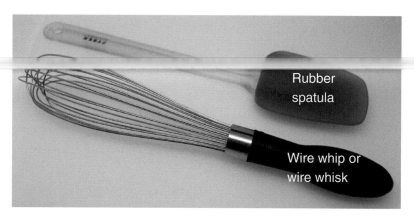

Measuring Tools

measuring cups: Cups with measurements (½ cup, ⅓ cup, etc.) on the sides and spouts for easy pouring.

measuring spoons: Used for measuring small amounts of foods such as spices. They come in a set of 1 tablespoon, ½ tablespoon, 1 teaspoon, ½ teaspoon, and ¼ teaspoon.

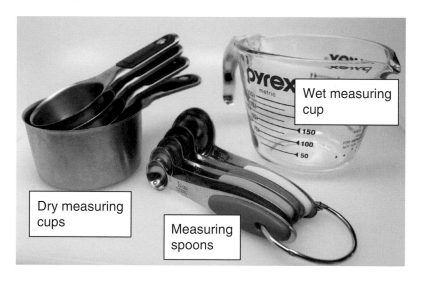

Additional Equipment

colander: A large perforated bowl used for rinsing food and draining pasta or other foods.

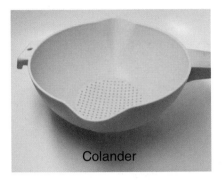
Colander

spatula: A flat metal or plastic tool used for lifting and turning meats, eggs, and other foods.

tongs: A tool with two arms that are used to pick up items, such as pasta or lettuce.

slotted spoon: A spoon with slots for draining liquid from food being served.

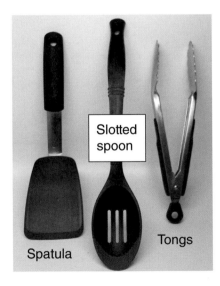
Slotted spoon

Tongs

Spatula

instant-read thermometer: A thermometer used to get temperature of foods.

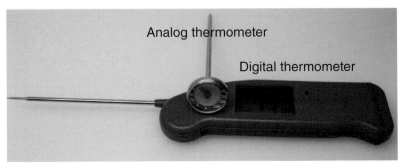
Analog thermometer

Digital thermometer

Safety Rules!

The kitchen can be a safe, or a very dangerous, part of your home. What's dangerous in your kitchen? Sharp knives, boiling water, steam, and hot oil are a few things. Always check with an adult before trying any of the recipes. Talk to them about what you are allowed to do by yourself and when you need an adult's assistance. And always follow these safety guidelines.

Around the Stove and Oven

- Get your parent's permission before using a stove or oven.

- Don't wear long, baggy shirts or sweaters when cooking. They could catch fire.

- Never turn your back on a frying pan that contains oil.

- Never fry with oil at a high temperature.

- Don't spray a pan with vegetable oil cooking spray over the stove or near heat. Oil will burn at high temperatures, so spray the pan over the sink.

- Always use pot holders or wear oven mitts when using the oven or handling something that is hot. Make sure your pot holders are not wet. Wet pot holders transmit the heat from the hot item you are holding directly to your skin.

Always wear oven mitts when using the oven.

- Don't overfill pans with boiling or simmering liquids.

- Open pan lids away from you to let steam escape safely.

Open pan lids away from you to
let steam escape.

- Keep pan handles turned away from the edge of the stove. The pans could be knocked off the stove and splatter hot food.

- Stir foods with long-handled spoons.

- Keep pets and small children away from hot stoves and ovens during cooking. (Try to keep them out of the kitchen altogether.)

- If a fire starts in a pan on the stove, you can smother it by covering it with the pan lid or pouring baking soda on it. Never use water to put out a fire in a pan with oil—it only makes a fire worse.

Using Appliances

- Only use an appliance that you know exactly how to operate.

- Never operate an appliance that is near the sink or sitting in water.

- Don't use frayed electrical cords or damaged plugs and outlets. Tell an adult.

Using a Microwave Oven

- Use only microwave-safe cookware, paper towels, paper plates, or paper cups. The best microwave dishes say "microwave safe" on the label. Don't use metal pans, aluminum foil, plastic foam containers, brown paper bags, plastic wrap, or margarine tubs in the microwave.

- Use pot holders to remove items.

- If a dish is covered, make sure there is some opening through which steam can escape during cooking.

- When taking foods out of the microwave, wait a minute and open the container so that steam escapes away from your hands and face.

- Prick foods like potatoes and hot dogs with a fork before putting them into the microwave.

- Never try to cook a whole egg in the microwave—it will burst!

Using a Knife

- Get your parent's permission before using any knife.

- Always pick up a knife by its handle.

- Pay attention to what you're doing!

- Cut away from the body and away from anyone near you.

- Use a sliding, back-and-forth motion when slicing foods with a knife.

- Don't leave a knife near the edge of a table. It can be easily knocked off, or a small child may touch it.

- Don't use knives to cut string or to open cans or bottles.

- Don't put a knife into a sink full of water. Instead, put it on the drainboard to avoid cuts.

Nutrition in a Nutshell

Nutrition is a science that looks at the calories and nutrients in food and beverages and how they affect your body and health. The energy in food is measured in units called **calories**. Your body needs energy to digest meals, engage in physical activity, and maintain the body. **Nutrients**, such as **fat** and **protein**, are the nourishing substances in foods that give you energy, allow your body to grow, and keep you feeling healthy. Other nutrients, such as vitamins and minerals, help regulate many processes that go on in your body, such as the beating of your heart. Water is the most important nutrient because you can survive only a few days without water. Water plays an important part in all processes in your body and accounts for about half of your body weight.

Following are some guidelines for eating a nutritious diet.

1. *Eat a variety of foods.* You need more than 40 different nutrients for good health.

2. *Eat plenty of vegetables, fruits, and whole grains* such as whole-wheat bread and brown rice. **Fiber**, a nutrient, is found only in plant foods such as vegetables, fruits, and grains. Eating fiber keeps your digestive tract healthy and is linked to lower body weight and reduced risk of colon cancer.

3. Use *MyPlate* (developed by the U.S. Department of Agriculture) to guide your food choices. When you have a meal, make half your plate vegetables and fruits, about one quarter grains, and one quarter protein, and include some dairy foods (such as milk or cheese).

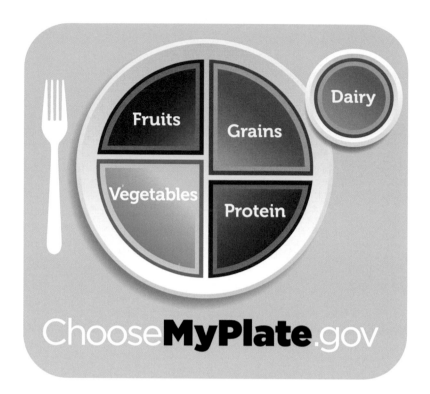

4. For meals and snacks, *choose whole foods* such as fresh fruits and vegetables, plain frozen vegetables, fresh or frozen meats and poultry, milk, eggs, and whole grains like brown rice, oats, and quinoa. **Whole foods** are generally not processed or refined and do not have any added ingredients, such as sugar. The more added sugars you consume, the more likely you are to be overweight and have other health issues such as heart disease and diabetes. Some whole foods, such as milk, are minimally processed to make it safe to drink.

5. For meals and snacks, *be moderate in how often you pick* **highly processed foods** such as cookies, candy, ice cream, sweetened breakfast cereals, many crackers and chips, luncheon meats and frankfurters, bottled salad dressings, and canned soups. These foods taste really good but they are usually low in fiber and high in added sugars and/or unhealthy fats.

Choose these highly processed foods in moderation.

6. *To have a healthy body and weight, children and adolescents should follow the 5–2–1–0 rule.*

   - Eat at least *five fruits and vegetables a day.*

   - Keep *screen time* (like TV, video games, computer) down to *2 hours or less per day.*

   - Get *1 hour or more of physical activity every day.*

   - *Drink 0 sugar-sweetened drinks.* Replace soft drinks, sports drinks, and even 100% fruit juice with milk or water.

Rules of the Game for Food Safety

Many different germs can contaminate foods and cause food poisoning, also called **foodborne illness**. When food is not handled in a safe manner, those germs can cause food poisoning. Symptoms of food poisoning include diarrhea, vomiting, upset stomach, or nausea. The four simple food safety steps in the poster will lower the chance that anyone in your family will get sick due to food poisoning.

RULES *of* the GAME
for Food Safety

Keep it clean

Before you eat or handle food, wash your hands, food prep tools and surfaces.

Cook to the right temperature

Use a food thermometer to check that foods are cooked to the right temperature: **165°F** for chicken and **160°F** for ground beef.

Watch the clock

Throw out perishable food that has been sitting at room temperature for more than two hours; one hour if it's **90°F** or warmer.

Serve at the right temperature

Keep hot foods at **140°F** or warmer, and cold foods at **40°F** or colder.

 **CDC**

www.cdc.gov/foodsafety

CS272887-B

Part 1

Questions, Questions, Questions!

Chapter 1

How Does Food Cook?

～～～～～～～～～～～～～～～～～～～～～

Some foods, such as fruits, can be eaten raw, but many foods must be cooked before eating. For example, raw meats and chicken often contain very small organisms (such as **bacteria**) that may be harmful, so most meats and poultry are cooked before eating. To cook food, you need a source of heat (such as the gas flames of an outdoor grill) that will transfer its heat to the food you want to cook. Heat is a form of energy and it will always move to a cooler substance.

Which Potato Cooks Faster?

Purpose: *To see and understand how heat is transferred to food.*

Procedure

1. Preheat the oven to 400°F (205°C).

2. Scrub the potatoes with a brush under running water. Pat dry. Remove any eyes or decayed areas with a paring knife on a cutting board.

3. Prick the skin of one potato with a fork.

4. Put on oven mitts and place the potato from step 3 on a rack in the middle of the oven. Bake until tender, 50–60 minutes. Remove using oven mitts. Pierce with a fork to see if it is tender. If not, put back into the oven for 3–5 more minutes. When done, write the cooking time in your *Science Chef Notebook*.

5. While the first potato bakes, put another potato into a medium saucepan. Put enough water into the pan to cover the potato.

6. Bring the water to a boil, then reduce the heat to low to simmer about 20 minutes. Use tongs to remove the potato from the water and place on a paper towel. Prick with a fork to determine if it is tender. If not, use the tongs to place back in the water for 3–5 minutes. Write the cooking time in your *Science Chef Notebook*.

Materials

3 Yukon Gold potatoes, similar size

scrub brush

paring knife

cutting board

fork

medium saucepan

tongs

7. Prick the final potato with a fork. Using high power in a microwave, cook 5–7 minutes. After microwaving, use a fork to determine if the potato is cooked enough. Microwave another minute if the potato is not yet very tender. Write the cooking time in your *Science Chef Notebook*.

Bake | Simmer | Microwave

Observations

Record the answers to these questions in your *Science Chef Notebook* (see "About This Book" for how to set up your own notebook).

1. How long did each potato (baked, boiled, microwaved) take to cook? Which potato took the most time to cook? Which potato took the least time to cook?

2. Which potato(es) were cooked by the movement of hot air or liquid?

3. Which potato(es) were cooked by radiation?

4. Which potato was the tastiest?

Heat Transfer and Cooking

Heat can be transferred to cook foods in one of three ways.

1. **Conduction** occurs when heat moves from something that is hot to something touching it. For example, if you put eggs into a hot frying pan, the eggs will start to cook.

2. **Convection** occurs when heat is spread by the movement of hot air, such as in an oven, or the movement of hot liquid, such as in a pot of boiling water. In an oven, hot air circulates around food and cooks it. Some ovens, called convection ovens, have a fan in them to force the air to circulate even faster and this speeds up the cooking process even more.

3. **Radiation** occurs when heat is transferred by waves—a form of energy that is all around us—as in sunlight or the glowing coals of a charcoal grill. Microwave ovens also transmit radiation waves. When these radiation waves are absorbed by foods, they cause the water **molecules** in the food to vibrate fast, which creates heat.

Whichever way a food is cooked, the larger the food, the longer it takes to cook.

What Happened in the Experiment?

Convection of hot air in the oven caused the potato to get hot and cook. When the potato was placed in the boiling water, heat transferred from the hot water to the cold potato (conduction) and the movement of the hot water (convection) also caused further cooking. The radiation in the microwave caused the water molecules in the potato to move faster and create heat.

The microwave oven cooked the potato the fastest because microwaves push almost 2 inches into the food. In an oven or in a pot of boiling water, the surface of the potato gets hot first, and then the potato cooks from the outside in, which is slower than in the microwave.

The oven cooked the potato slower than the simmering water, yet the air in the oven was hotter than the simmering water. This is because simmering water transfers heat a lot better than hot air does. For example, if you put your hand into a 400 °F (205 °C) oven (without touching anything) for a moment, you will not burn yourself. But if you put your hand into simmering water (about 200 °F), you will burn yourself.

So which potato tasted the best? That is really a matter of personal taste. But if you like a crispy skin, you surely liked the baked potato from the oven best. The dry air in an oven dries out the potato skin and a dry skin is crispy. You don't get that effect when cooking in boiling water or in the microwave, which results in a softer moist skin.

Basic Baked Potatoes

Baked potatoes are one of the easiest foods to make.
Just wash 'em, fork 'em, and bake 'em.

Difficulty: Beginner / **Time:** 10 minutes plus 50–60 minutes to bake / **Makes:** 6 potatoes

Ingredients

6 medium baking potatoes (such as russet or Yukon Gold potatoes)

½ cup low-fat sour cream or plain yogurt

Optional toppings: finely chopped fresh chives or fresh dill, bacon bits, shredded cheese

Steps

1. Preheat the oven to 400 °F (205 °C).

2. Scrub the potatoes with a brush under running water. Pat dry with a paper towel. Remove any eyes or decayed areas with a knife.

3. Prick the skins with a fork. This gives the steam that will develop inside the potato a chance to escape. Otherwise, the potato might explode.

4. Put on oven mitts and place the potatoes on a rack in the middle of the oven. Bake until tender, 50–60 minutes. Use oven mitts to remove from the oven. Fork a potato to make sure it is tender and cooked.

5. Using a knife on a cutting board, split each potato down the middle. Place on a plate and top with low-fat sour cream or plain yogurt. If desired, top with finely chopped fresh chives or fresh dill, bacon bits, or shredded cheese.

Variation

To microwave potatoes instead of baking them, follow steps 1–3. Arrange the potatoes on a microwavable plate and allow 1 inch of space between potatoes. Avoid placing one potato in the middle surrounded by the others, because the potato in the middle will cook much more slowly. Use high power and cook 5–7 minutes for 1 potato, 7–8 minutes for 2 potatoes, and 10–14 minutes for 4 potatoes. After microwaving, use a fork to determine if the potato is cooked enough. Microwave another minute if a potato is not yet very tender.

When cleaning potatoes, cut out any green areas (they can make you sick).

Broccoli and Cheddar Stuffed Potatoes

To make stuffed potatoes, bake the potatoes first. Then scoop out the white of the potato and mix with additional ingredients. Now you are ready to bake the potatoes again. That's why we also call them "twice baked."

Difficulty: Intermediate / **Time:** 70 minutes / **Makes:** 6 stuffed potatoes

Ingredients

6 medium baking potatoes (such as russet or Yukon Gold potatoes)

1 bunch fresh broccoli

½ cup low-fat milk

4 oz cheddar cheese, shredded

⅛ teaspoon pepper

4 oz cheddar cheese, shredded

Steps

1. Prepare the potatoes using the Basic Baked Potatoes recipe.

2. While the potatoes are baking, use a knife to cut off the broccoli florets on a cutting board.

3. Put the broccoli florets in a steaming basket. Wash them well under running water. Place the steaming basket in a saucepan with enough water in it to just reach the bottom of the basket.

4. Put the saucepan on a burner. Set to high heat and reduce heat once water boils. Steam the broccoli for about 10 minutes.

5. Let the broccoli cool, then chop it into smaller pieces using a knife on a cutting board.

6. Use oven mitts to remove the potatoes from the oven. Push a fork into each potato to make sure it is tender. Let potatoes cool for 5–10 minutes.

7. Using a knife, slice off the top of each potato and scoop the white pulp into a large bowl. Mash the potato pulp with a fork.

8. Add the broccoli, milk, 4 oz of shredded cheddar cheese, and pepper to the potato pulp. Mix with a spoon.

9. Stuff the mixture back into the potatoes. Sprinkle with remaining cheddar cheese. Place the potatoes on a cookie sheet as in photo.

10. Put the cookie sheet into the oven and cook the potatoes for about 10 minutes or until the cheese is bubbly.

Broccoli florets are the tightly packed heads of tiny buds on top of stalks.

Variations

Riced Cauliflower and Cheese Stuffed Potatoes: Substitute 10 oz fresh or frozen riced cauliflower for the broccoli.

Mexican Chili Stuffed Potatoes: Substitute canned or homemade chili with beans for the broccoli.

Vegetable Cheese Stuffed Potatoes: Substitute 10 oz of any fresh or frozen vegetable for the broccoli. If using frozen, thaw the frozen vegetable in the refrigerator 1 day prior to making the recipe. If the vegetable is larger than a pea or corn niblet, you may want to chop the vegetable before adding it to the potato pulp.

Smashed Potatoes

This recipe is for a traditional American favorite, mashed potatoes.

Difficulty: Intermediate / **Time:** 40 minutes / **Makes:** 4 ½-cup servings

Ingredients

2 medium boiling potatoes

2 tablespoons vegetable oil spread, olive oil, or butter

¼ cup low-fat milk

dash salt

Steps

1. Scrub the potatoes with a brush under running water and pat dry with a paper towel. Remove the eyes and any decayed areas with a paring knife on a cutting board.

2. Peel the potatoes. Then cut each potato into quarters.

3. Put the potatoes in the saucepan and cover them with water. Bring water to a boil over medium-high heat. Then simmer the potatoes until tender, about 20–30 minutes.

4. Using a colander, drain the water and put the potatoes in a large bowl.

5. Mash the potatoes with a potato masher or electric mixer.

6. Add vegetable oil spread, olive oil, or butter, along with the milk and salt to the potatoes. Use more milk for thinner smashed potatoes and less milk for thicker mashed potatoes.

Variations

Garlic Smashed Potatoes: Add one tablespoon chopped garlic to fat, milk, and salt.

Smashed Spinach Potatoes: Add 1 cup of frozen and thawed chopped spinach to mashed potatoes.

"Shroomy" Smashed Potatoes: Add 4-oz can sliced mushrooms to mashed potatoes.

When a potato is cooked in water, its starch granules absorb moisture so they swell in size and soften in texture.

Cook potatoes for mashing at a simmer (not a boil) so the starch doesn't absorb too much moisture.

Air-Fried French Fries

Homemade French fries using an air fryer are easy to make and still crispy without using a lot of oil.

Difficulty: Intermediate / **Time:** 25 minutes to prepare plus 10–12 minutes to cook / **Makes:** 4 servings

Ingredients

2 large baking potatoes

2 tablespoons olive oil

1 tablespoon arrowroot

¼ teaspoon garlic powder

seasoned salt, to taste

Steps

1. Preheat oven to 400 °F (205 °C).

2. Scrub the potatoes with a brush under running water and pat dry with a paper towel. Remove the eyes and any decayed areas with a knife.

3. Peel the potatoes if you like (but the peels taste good, too!).

4. Using a knife on a cutting board, slice the potatoes into ¼-inch slices. Then cut each slice into matchstick-sized pieces (about 1¼ inches square by 2½ inches long).

5. Put the potato pieces into a large bowl of water to prevent them from turning brown before the next step.

6. When all the potatoes are cut, drain the water from the bowl. Place the potatoes in a zipper lock bag with the olive oil, arrowroot, and garlic powder. Close the bag and shake until all potatoes are coated.

7. Place the potatoes in the air fryer. Turn the air fryer to 400 °F (205 °C). Set the timer to air fry the potatoes for 10 minutes.

8. Check and fry for an additional 2 minutes for extra crispy French fries. Sprinkle with seasoned salt and toss before serving.

Variation

Southwestern Sweet Potato Fries: Use 2 large sweet potatoes instead of baking potatoes. Once the potatoes are cut and drained, place in a zipper lock bag with 2 tablespoons olive oil, 1 teaspoon cumin, and 1 teaspoon chili powder. Once cooked, sprinkle with cayenne pepper and then salt to taste.

Overloading the fryer's basket will slow down cooking and give you soggy fries.

As potatoes grow underground, they store up starch, an excellent source of energy.

Potato Skins with Cheddar and Salsa

Potato skins are a popular appetizer. Skins are served with only a little potato pulp left in the skin.

Difficulty: Intermediate / **Time:** 1½ hours / **Makes:** 16 skins, 4 skins/serving

Ingredients

4 large baking potatoes

¾ cup grated cheddar cheese

½ cup salsa

1 teaspoon dried parsley

Steps

1. Preheat oven to 400 °F (205 °C).

2. Scrub the potatoes with a brush under running water and pat dry with a paper towel. Remove the eyes and any decayed areas with a paring knife. Prick the potato skins with a fork.

3. Place the potatoes on a rack in the middle of the oven and bake until tender, about 50–60 minutes.

4. Remove potatoes from the oven. Using a knife on a cutting board, cut potatoes in half lengthwise. Let cool.

5. When cool enough to handle, scrape the white pulp of each potato half into a bowl, leave a thin layer of pulp on the skins.

6. Cut each skin into two pieces and sprinkle with cheddar cheese. Then top each skin with 1½ teaspoons salsa. Place the skins on a cookie sheet.

7. Put the cookie sheet into the oven and cook the skins for about 12–15 minutes, or until the cheese is bubbly. Sprinkle with parsley flakes before serving.

You can use the discarded white pulp to make mashed potatoes.

Crunchy Country Potato Salad

Difficulty: Advanced / **Time:** 1 hour / **Makes:** 8 servings

Steps

1. Scrub the potatoes with a brush under running water and pat dry with a paper towel. Remove the eyes and any decayed areas with a paring knife on a cutting board.

2. Place the potatoes in a 4-quart pot and boil for 12–15 minutes until tender. Drain potatoes with a colander and cool for 30 minutes.

3. While the potatoes cool, wash off the celery and pat dry with a paper towel.

4. Use a paring knife to cut the celery stalks in half lengthwise on a cutting board. Then, cut each half into ¼-inch long pieces. Place celery pieces in a large bowl.

5. Remove the outer skin of the onion. Slice the onion in half. Put one half aside. Cut the onion half into three pieces and then chop. Wrap the unused onion and store in the refrigerator. Add onion to the celery pieces.

6. Place the pickle spears on the cutting board. Cut each spear lengthwise and then cut each strip into quarter inch pieces. Add to the onion and celery mixture and toss as shown in photo.

7. Using a paring knife, place the potatoes on a cutting board and cut into quarters. Add potatoes to the onion and celery mixture.

Ingredients

2 pounds baby red potatoes

2 stalks celery

1 small red onion

2 dill pickle spears

¾ cup low fat mayonnaise

2 tablespoons yellow mustard

1 tablespoon dried dill

1 teaspoon salt

1 teaspoon dried parsley and paprika for garnish

8. Add the mayonnaise, mustard, dill, and salt to the potatoes. Mix together until the ingredients are thoroughly blended.

9. Serve potato salad on a platter and garnish with dried parsley and paprika.

Compared to other potatoes, red potatoes are low in starch so they don't get mushy, which would be bad in potato salad.

Create-a-Potato Party

Invite some friends for a potato supper party and see how creative they can be in making their own potato main dish.

Difficulty: Intermediate / **Time:** 10 minutes preparation +1 hour cooking +30 minutes to finish / **Makes:** 4 servings

Steps

1. Preheat oven to 400 °F (205 °C).

2. Scrub the potatoes with a brush under running water and pat dry with a paper towel. Remove the eyes and any decayed areas with a paring knife. Prick the potato skins with a fork.

3. Place the potatoes on a rack in the middle of the oven and bake until tender, about 50–60 minutes. Let cool enough to handle.

4. While the potatoes cook, choose which type of potatoe(s) you want to make and get the ingredients ready.

5. Once tender, remove the potatoes from the oven with oven mitts and let cool 10 minutes.

6. Using a knife on a cutting board, cut each potato in half lengthwise. Use a spoon to scoop the pulp into a large bowl.

7. Add milk to the potatoes and mash the mixture with a hand masher. Combine fillings with the mashed potatoes to make whichever stuffed potatoes you have chosen.

8. When the potatoes are stuffed, put them on a cookie sheet and bake them in the oven for 12–15 minutes.

Fillings

Southwestern Potato (shown at left in photo): Cooked ground beef, diced tomato, and grated cheddar cheese.

Hawaiian Potato (shown in middle in photo): Diced cooked ham, raisins, and grated muenster cheese. Top with pineapple chunks.

Ingredients

2 large baking potatoes

2–3 tablespoons skim or low-fat milk

Take-Me-Out-to-the-Ballgame Potato (shown at right in photo): Hot dog slices, baked beans, and grated cheddar cheese.

Popeye Potato: Cooked chicken cubes, chopped spinach, and grated Swiss cheese.

Middle-Eastern Potato: Bulgur (whole-wheat grain that has been cooked, dried, and cracked into small pieces), sliced tomatoes, grated Swiss cheese, and chopped walnuts. To cook bulgur, put 1 cup in a saucepan with 2½ cups water and cook over low heat about 20–25 minutes.

Make sure the inside of the potato has cooled off before scooping out the pulp.

You only need a small amount of the fillings ingredients.

Quinoa-and-Salsa-Stuffed Sweet Potatoes with Awesome Avocado Sauce

Difficulty: Advanced / **Time:** 1¼ hours / **Makes:** 4 servings

Steps

1. Preheat oven to 400 °F (205 °C).

2. Scrub the potatoes with a brush under running water and pat dry with a paper towel. Remove the eyes and any decayed areas with a knife. Prick the skins with a fork.

3. Place the potatoes in the middle of the oven and bake until tender, 50–60 minutes.

4. While the potatoes bake, place the quinoa in a strainer basket and rinse.

5. Place the quinoa in a medium saucepan over low heat and lightly toast for about 2 minutes. Turn off the heat.

6. Add the vegetable broth, salt, cumin, chili powder, and lime juice to the quinoa.

7. Turn the heat to medium and bring the quinoa mixture to a simmer. Turn the burner to low and cover the quinoa. Cook covered for 20 minutes. Set aside.

8. While the quinoa cooks, prepare the avocado sauce (recipe follows).

9. Using a knife on a cutting board, slice the onion in half. Put one half aside. Cut the onion half into three pieces and then chop. Wrap the unused onion and place in the refrigerator.

10. Use oven mitts to remove the potatoes once tender. Using a knife and cutting board, split the potato down the center. Pinch the ends together to allow room for the fillings.

Ingredients

4 large sweet potatoes

1 cup dried quinoa

2 cups vegetable broth

½ teaspoon salt

½ teaspoon cumin

½ teaspoon chili powder

2 tablespoons lime juice

½ whole large red onion (¾ cup chopped)

1 cup salsa

lime slices

tortilla chips (optional)

11. To assemble the potatoes, place three tablespoons of salsa in the bottom of each potato. Fill with cooked quinoa. Sprinkle with red onions and remaining salsa if desired. Drizzle with the avocado sauce before serving.

12. Garnish with lime slices and serve with tortilla chips if desired.

Awesome Avocado Sauce

Steps

1. Using a cutting board and a knife, cut the avocado in half and pull apart. Pull out the pit in the center. Squeeze each half of the avocado to release the fruit from the skin. Place the fruit in the blender.

2. Snip the stems off the parsley with scissors. Pull the leaves off the stem and place in blender.

3. Roll the limes on a countertop to loosen the membranes. Cut the limes in half. Squeeze each lime half over the blender to collect the juice.

4. Add the olive oil, water, cumin, chili powder, and salt to the blender and blend until smooth. Pour sauce over the potatoes and serve.

Ingredients

1 ripe avocado

¾ cup chopped fresh parsley

3 limes, juiced

2 tablespoons olive oil

1 cup water

½ teaspoon cumin

¼ teaspoon chili powder

¼ teaspoon salt

Quinoa is a nutritious grain like rice that is cooked in water.

Video at http://www.wiley.com/go/sciencechef.

Chapter 2

Why Does Popcorn Pop?

~~~~~~

Have you ever wondered what would happen if you put uncooked kernels of corn from corn on the cob into the microwave? Would they pop and make great popcorn? The bad news is that they would just make a mess of your microwave. The good news is that popcorn, whose proper name is popping corn, is a special breed of corn that will explode to 30–40 times its original size when you heat it.

How Do You Get the Most Pops?

Purpose: *To understand how popcorn pops.*

Procedure

1. Place ½ cup popcorn on cookie sheet and leave in an oven at 200 °F for 60 minutes. Then let cool for 10 minutes.

2. Place ½ cup popcorn in bowl with 1 cup water for 60 minutes. After 60 minutes, drain the popcorn in a colander.

3. Leave ½ cup popcorn in a plastic bag for 60 minutes.

Materials

1½ cups unpopped popcorn

cookie sheet

medium bowl

plastic sandwich bag

colander

frying pan, lid, and vegetable oil

or

hot-air popcorn popper

Soak it!

Bake it!

Bag it!

4. Pop each of the three batches of popcorn separately. You can use a hot-air popper or the following recipe for The Best Popcorn.

Observations

Record the answers to these questions in your *Science Chef Notebook* (see "About This Book" for how to set up your own notebook).

1. Which batch of popcorn made the biggest kernels of popcorn? Which batch made the smallest kernels?

2. Using a measuring cup, measure and record how much popcorn each batch made.

3. Which batch made the most popcorn? Name one factor that may have contributed to this.

4. Which batch made the least popcorn? Name one factor that may have contributed to this.

Popcorn Science

Popping corn is the only type of corn to actually pop. The secret to its pop is a drop of water found in each kernel. As each kernel is heated, the drop of water turns to **steam**. The steam's energy ultimately breaks the hard kernel, and out pops popcorn! When water goes from being a liquid to a gas, it is called a phase change. A **phase change** is a change from one state (solid, liquid, or gas) to another without a change in chemical composition.

Phase changes require a lot of energy. The energy in steam is almost 10 times greater than the energy in the same weight of boiling water. So, keep your hands and arms away from steam to avoid a serious skin burn.

Popcorn is a great snack that is easy to make, fun to eat, and low in fat. It is a whole grain and a great source of **fiber**, a nutrient that helps keep your digestive tract healthy. Depending on how you make your popcorn and what you add to it, you can have a snack with a lot of, or just a little, fat.

Three ways to pop your popcorn are in a hot-air popper made especially for that purpose, in hot oil using almost any type of pan, or in the microwave using specially packaged microwave popcorn. You can buy popcorn with either white or yellow kernels. White corn pops up fluffier than yellow corn, but most popcorn sold in the United States is yellow corn because it tastes better.

What Happened in the Experiment?

The popcorn that was soaked in water made the biggest kernels of popped popcorn as well as the largest amount of popcorn. This is because the soaking process added water to the kernel. The more water there is, the more steam is created in cooking, making the kernels pop better.

The popcorn that was dried out in the oven lost most of that drop of water that turns to steam during popping. The dried popcorn kernels made smaller kernels of popped popcorn and were more likely to be duds. Therefore, they produced the smallest amount of popped popcorn.

The popcorn that was left in a plastic bag made medium-sized kernels of popped popcorn and an average amount, as it was neither dried nor soaked.

The Best Popcorn

If you don't have a frying pan for this recipe, you can use a stockpot, a Dutch oven, or even a wok.

Difficulty: Beginner / **Time:** 10 minutes / **Makes:** 5 2-cup servings

Ingredients

2 tablespoons vegetable oil

½ cup unpopped popcorn kernels

Steps

1. Preheat the frying pan by placing it on the burner and setting the heat to medium for 2 minutes.

2. Add the oil.

3. Put one kernel into the frying pan and heat. When the kernel pops, you will know that the oil is at the right temperature.

4. Remove the pan from the heat and pour in the rest of the kernels in the pan. Shake the pan to distribute the kernels evenly. Cover the pan and put it back on the heat.

5. Once it starts popping, tip the lid a little to allow steam to escape. Also shake the pan back and forth just above the burner, so each kernel is heated evenly and does not burn.

6. Continue to shake until the popping slows to about one pop every few seconds. Then remove from heat immediately. Turn the burner off.

7. Wait a moment and slowly remove the lid away from you so the steam escapes without touching you. Let the popcorn cool for a minute, then pour in a large bowl.

Variation

Air Popped Popcorn: Use ¼ cup unpopped corn kernels. Place in air popper. Place a large mixing bowl under the chute where the popcorn pops out. Turn the machine on until all the kernels are popped.

Carefully measure the popcorn or it will be popping all over the kitchen.

Don't substitute butter or margarine for the vegetable oil as they will burn in the hot frying pan.

"New" Fashioned Kettle Corn

Old-fashioned kettle corn was made in a large cast-iron kettle for festive occasions such as fairs. As the popcorn cooked, fat and sugar were added resulting in a sweet treat. In our "new" version, you will add butter and sugar to the popped popcorn.

Difficulty: Beginner / **Time:** 10 minutes / **Makes:** 5 2-cup servings

Ingredients

¼ cup butter or vegetable oil spread

10 cups popped popcorn (made by popping ½ cup popcorn kernels)

¼ cup white sugar (or brown sugar, see Variation)

1 teaspoon salt

Brown sugar gets its color from molasses, a thick syrup made during the sugar-making process that is bittersweet.

Steps

1. Place the popcorn in a large bowl.

2. Place butter or vegetable oil spread in the microwave dish and cover with lid. Cook on high for 30–60 seconds until melted and bubbly.

3. Let cool for 1 minute before removing cover.

4. Pour over the popcorn. Then, add the sugar and salt to the popcorn and toss gently.

Variation

Caramel Kettle Corn: Instead of using white sugar, toss with ¼ cup brown sugar.

Popcorn Power Bars

If you like dried fruit and peanuts, try this recipe! It's a great packable snack, too.

Difficulty: Beginner / **Time:** 20 minutes to prepare plus 2 hours to set / **Makes:** 24 squares

Steps

1. Preheat the frying pan by placing it on the burner and setting the heat to medium for 2 minutes.

2. Add the butter or vegetable oil spread. Once melted, reduce the heat to low and add the marshmallows.

3. Stir constantly until the marshmallows are melted, about 2 minutes.

4. Add the honey and vanilla extract and stir well. Remove the mixture from the heat and turn off the burner.

5. Let the mixture cool for 5 minutes.

6. Add the warm mixture to a large bowl filled with popped popcorn.

7. Add the raisins, cranberries, and peanuts, stirring constantly until the popcorn is coated.

8. Spray a cookie sheet (with sides) with vegetable oil cooking spray.

9. Pour the popcorn mixture onto the sheet and press it down. If the mixture gets too sticky, wet your hands with cold water.

Ingredients

¼ cup butter or vegetable oil spread

10½ oz bag mini-marshmallows

¼ cup honey

1 teaspoon vanilla extract

10 cups popped popcorn (made by popping ½ cup popcorn kernels)

¾ cup raisins

½ cup dried cranberries

¾ cup roasted peanuts

vegetable oil cooking spray

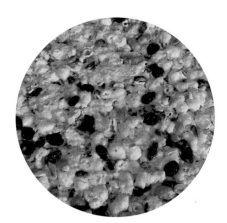

10. Allow the mixture to set in the sheet for 2 hours. Then cut with a serrated knife into bars.

Long ago, people made marshmallows using a thick, gooey substance from the roots of a marshmallow plant.

A serrated knife looks like it has teeth that prevent the food being cut from getting squashed.

Trail Mix Popcorn

This is a great snack to pack for bike rides, hiking, and other outdoor activities.

Difficulty: Beginner / **Time:** 15 minutes / **Makes:** 18 1-cup servings

Steps

1. Measure the ingredients one at a time and put them into a large bowl.

2. Toss all the ingredients together. To keep Trail Mix Popcorn fresh, put it in plastic bags.

Ingredients

10 cups popped popcorn (made by popping ⅓ cup popcorn kernels)

3 cups pretzel sticks

2 cups Wheat Chex® cereal

1 cup Corn Chex cereal

1 cup raisins

½ cup sunflower seeds

½ cup sliced almonds

"Movie Time" Cheddar Cheese and Chive Popcorn

This recipe combines popcorn with cheddar cheese and chives for a unique flavor. Chives are an herb from the same family as onions. They have long, green leaves that look like skinny tubes and have a mild oniony flavor.

Difficulty: Beginner / **Time:** 15 minutes / **Makes:** 5 2-cup servings

Ingredients

¼ cup butter or vegetable oil spread

⅓ cup grated cheddar cheese

10 cups popped popcorn (made by popping ½ cup popcorn kernels)

1 bunch fresh chives

or

2 tablespoons dried chives

> When a fresh herb (like chives) is cut, chewed, or heated, it releases its flavor. Each herb's flavor comes from a number of chemical compounds in the plant.

Steps

1. Place butter or vegetable oil spread in a microwave dish and cover with lid. Cook on high for 30–60 seconds until melted and bubbly.

2. Let cool for 1 minute before removing cover.

3. Add the grated cheese to the melted butter and stir until the cheese is melted.

4. Pour the butter-cheese mixture over the popcorn in a large bowl and toss until all the popcorn is coated.

5. If using fresh chives, wash, drain, and chop them to make ¼ cup.

6. Toss the fresh or dried chives with the popcorn mixture and serve immediately.

Popcorn Santa Fe

This recipe is inspired by the cooking of the southwestern United States. Southwestern cooking uses some spicy seasonings such as cumin and chili powder.

Difficulty: Beginner / **Time:** 20 minutes / **Makes:** 24 squares

Steps

1. Preheat the oven to 350 °F.

2. Preheat a frying pan by placing on a burner and setting heat to medium for 2 minutes. Add the butter to the frying pan. Once the butter is melted, add the ½ cup grated cheese and stir until the cheese is melted. Turn the burner off and set the frying pan on an empty burner. Let the mixture cool for 5 minutes.

3. Add the butter-cheese mixture to the popcorn in a large bowl and toss until the popcorn is coated.

4. Add the salt, cumin, and chili powder to the popcorn and toss again.

5. Spray a cookie sheet (with sides) with vegetable oil cooking spray. Spread the popcorn mixture on the cookie sheet.

6. Sprinkle the popcorn with the remaining ⅔ cup grated cheese. Spoon on salsa. The salsa will not cover all of the popcorn—just add small spoonfuls here and there.

7. Bake in the oven for 2–3 minutes or until the cheese has barely melted.

8. Remove the popcorn from the cookie sheet with a spatula. Serve the popcorn on top of a large platter of nacho chips with extra salsa if you like.

Ingredients

¼ cup butter or vegetable oil spread

½ cup grated cheddar cheese

10 cups popped popcorn (made by popping ½ cup popcorn kernels)

1 teaspoon salt

½ teaspoon cumin powder

¼ teaspoon chili powder

vegetable oil cooking spray

⅔ cup grated cheddar cheese

½ cup salsa

10 oz bag nacho chips

Salsa originated in Mexico and there are many types. Salsa fresca is shown in the photo and is made from chopped tomatoes, onions, chile peppers, cilantro, and lime juice.

Springtime Pastel Popcorn Treats

Wrap these popcorn balls with pastel-colored cellophane wrap, and tie up with curling ribbon for a springtime holiday treat. Use the same recipe to make holiday popcorn balls to hang as decorations or give as gifts. Use red, green, or blue cellophane wrap and curling ribbon.

Difficulty: Intermediate / **Time:** 20 minutes to prepare plus 1 hour to refrigerate / **Makes:** 12 popcorn balls

Steps

1. Preheat the frying pan by placing it on a burner and setting the heat to medium for 2 minutes.

2. Add the butter or vegetable oil spread to the frying pan. Once melted, reduce the heat to low. Add the marshmallows and stir.

3. When the marshmallows are melted, add the honey and stir until melted.

4. Turn the burner off and set the frying pan on a cold burner. Let the mixture cool for 5 minutes.

5. Add the melted warm mixture to the popcorn in the large bowl and toss until the popcorn is coated.

6. Add dried cranberries, currants, coconut, and almonds to the popcorn mixture and mix thoroughly.

7. Moisten your hands with water. Take about ¾ cup of the popcorn mixture and pack it into a ball. Repeat until you have used up all the popcorn.

Ingredients

½ cup butter or vegetable oil spread

10½ oz bag marshmallows

¼ cup honey

10 cups popped popcorn using frying pan or air popper method

½ cup dried cranberries

½ cup dried currants

½ cup shredded coconut

¼ cup almond slices

8. Place the balls on a cookie sheet. Cover them loosely with plastic wrap and refrigerate for 1 hour.

9. Wrap popcorn in pastel-colored cellophane and tie with decorative ribbons.

Dried currants look like small raisins and taste sweet and tangy.

Video at http://www.wiley.com/go/sciencechef.

Chapter 3

Why Do Onions Make You Cry?

~~~~~~~~~~~~~~~~~~~~~~~~~~~~~~~~~~~~~

Did you ever notice someone crying when cutting or chopping onions? Did you think this person was just having a bad day? Well, the truth is that when you cut into an onion, the onion's cells open up and **enzymes** called allinases are released. These enzymes convert another molecule in the onion into an acid. Then the acid spontaneously rearranges itself to form a gas that stings your eyes. Nerves in your eyes detect the harmful gas and carry a signal for the eye to tear or cry because tears will flush out the irritating substance. Over the years, people have tried many tricks to keep their eyes from tearing. Unfortunately, most of these tricks don't work. Try the following experiment to see what really works.

How Can I Cut Onions Without Crying?

Purpose: *To test how to prevent your eyes from tearing when cutting onions.*

Materials

1 onion

knife

cutting board

swim goggles or scuba mask

cheese or matchstick

Procedure

1. Remove the outer, papery skin from the onion.

2. Put on safety goggles or a scuba mask.

3. On a cutting board, use a knife to cut the onion in half. Lay one part of the onion down flat on the cutting board, then slice the onion. Remove the goggles or mask.

4. Next, put a piece of cheese or matchstick between your teeth. Lay the other part of the onion down flat on the cutting board and slice. Remove the cheese or matchstick.

Observations

Record the answers to these questions in your *Science Chef Notebook* (see the "About This Book" section for how to set up your own notebook).

1. Did your eyes tear up when you put on the swimming goggles or a snorkel mask?

2. Did your eyes tear up when you put the cheese or matchstick between your teeth?

3. What is the best way to avoid tearing when slicing onions and why do you think it is effective?

Onions and Enzymes

Enzymes are present in the cells of fruits and vegetables and also in the cells of your body. They are made from **amino acids**, which are linked together in a unique arrangement. Amino acids are the building blocks of protein. A primary job of enzymes is to speed up chemical reactions in the cells. Enzymes are quite important in the process in which fruits become ripe. When vegetables, such as onions, are heated, their enzymes become inactive as heat disrupts the shape of the amino acids.

Bulb onions can be divided into categories by their color: yellow, white, or red. Yellow onions have a sharp flavor and they are widely used in cooking. White

onions are the classic onion used in Mexican cooking. Red onions have a mild flavor so they are a favorite in salads and sandwiches. In addition to these onions, there are sweet onions, which vary from yellow to white in color and are much sweeter than other onions. Sweet onions have names such as Vidalia (grown in and around Vidalia, Georgia) and Maui (grown on the island of Maui, Hawaii).

What Happened in the Experiment?

The only thing that works to completely shield your eyes from the vapors is to wear swimming goggles or a snorkel mask that covers your eyes. Without eye protection, you can *reduce* the amount of tears by chilling the onions for 30 minutes before cutting, slicing the onions under water, or slicing them under a fan that pulls the air away from you. The matchstick and cheese do not offer any help.

"A Plus" Air-Fried Onion Rings

Onion rings and French fries are most often cooked in a deep fryer surrounded by hot oil. Air fryers work by using superheated air to cook the fries on all sides. You can use a little oil in an air fryer if you want, but it is not necessary.

Difficulty: Intermediate / **Time:** 20 minutes to prepare +10 minutes to cook / **Makes:** 4 servings

Steps

1. Remove the outer, papery skin from the onion.

2. On a cutting board, use a knife and cut the onion into ½-inch rings. Place the rings on a plate in the refrigerator while making the batter.

3. Mix the flour, salt, and paprika together in a small bowl.

4. In another small bowl, combine the egg, milk, and lemon juice. Whisk lightly with a fork.

5. In a third small bowl, add the breadcrumbs.

6. Dip an onion ring into the flour mixture, then dip into the milk mixture. Dip the onion ring into the breadcrumbs, making sure each onion is evenly covered with crumbs. Repeat this process with the remaining onion rings.

7. Place the onions in the basket of the air fryer. Onions can be stacked on top of each other.

Ingredients

1 large onion

¾ cup flour

½ teaspoon salt

¼ teaspoon paprika

1 egg

1 cup low-fat (2%) or nonfat milk

2 tablespoons lemon juice

1 cup seasoned breadcrumbs

Foods that are air fried have fewer calories (energy) than deep-fat fried foods because deep-fat fried foods absorb oil in cooking.

Video at http://www.wiley.com/go/sciencechef.

8. Set the air fryer for 10 minutes at 380 °F (195 °C). Check when finished. For crispier onion rings, fry the onions for an additional 2 minutes. Serve with ketchup or your favorite sauce.

Variation

Oven-Baked Onion Rings: Preheat the onion to 425 °F (220 °C). Place onions on a nonstick mat, or spray a baking sheet with an olive oil spray. Bake the onion rings for 15 minutes until crispy.

Cheesy Cauliflower and Onion Bake

Cooking butter (a fat) and flour together in step 8 coats the flour particles with fat so you don't get lumps in your cheese sauce. The starch in flour swells rapidly in water and easily forms lumps if not coated with fat.

Difficulty: Advanced / **Time:** 35 minutes to prepare +15 minutes to bake / **Makes:** 8 side dishes

Steps

1. Preheat the oven to 350 °F (175 °C).

2. On a cutting board using a knife, cut the cauliflower into bite-sized florets.

3. Place the florets in a colander and wash under cold running water. Once rinsed, place into a vegetable steamer basket.

4. Place 1 inch of water into the bottom of a medium saucepan. Bring the water to a boil. Place the steamer basket over the boiling water and cover with a lid. Turn the heat to simmer. Steam the cauliflower for 8 minutes.

5. While the cauliflower cooks, remove the outer, papery skin from the onion. On a cutting board, use a knife to cut the onion in half. Lay each onion half flat on the cutting board and chop into small pieces.

6. Spoon the steamed cauliflower into a bowl and set aside to cool.

7. Preheat a skillet by placing on a burner and set to medium heat for 1 minute. Add olive oil to the pan. Add the onions and sauté for about 5 minutes until golden brown and tender. Turn off the heat and cool for a minute before adding the onions to the cauliflower.

8. To make the cheese sauce, preheat a saucepan on a burner set to medium heat for 2 minutes. Add the butter and melt. Then add the flour to the pan. Cook the butter and flour over medium heat, stirring constantly with a whisk for two or so minutes until bubbly. Do not let the mixture brown.

Ingredients

1 large head cauliflower

1 small onion

1 tablespoon olive oil

3 tablespoons butter (or vegetable oil spread)

3 tablespoons flour

1½ cups low-fat (2%) milk

¼ teaspoon nutmeg

¼ teaspoon salt

⅛ teaspoon cayenne pepper

1 tablespoon mustard

⅔ cup shredded cheddar cheese

1 tablespoon seasoned breadcrumbs

1 tablespoon dried parsley flakes

Variation

Cheesy Brussels Sprouts and Onion Bake: Substitute two pounds of Brussels sprouts for the cauliflower florets. Wash the Brussels sprouts. Peel off the outermost layer of leaves. With a cutting board and knife, cut off the root end of the Brussels sprouts, and then cut in half lengthwise. Proceed as above.

> **Cauliflower florets are the tightly packed heads of tiny buds on top of stalks.**
>
> **A ramekin is a ceramic dish that holds individual servings of food, such as macaroni and cheese, to be cooked in the oven.**

9. Slowly pour the milk into the butter and flour mixture, stirring constantly. Bring the milk mixture to a simmer, stirring constantly for 2–3 minutes.

10. Add the nutmeg, salt, pepper, mustard, and cheddar cheese. Continue to stir until melted. Turn off the heat. Pour the cheese sauce over the cauliflower and onions and toss lightly.

11. Divide the mixture between three 12 oz or four 8 oz au gratin dishes, or 8 individual oven-safe ramekins.

12. Sprinkle cauliflower and onion mixture with the breadcrumbs and parsley.

13. Place the dishes on a cookie sheet. Bake the cauliflower and onion mixture for 15 minutes at 350 °F (175 °C) until bubbly.

Chapter 4

Why Does Toast Brown?

~~~~~~

Did you ever wonder what happens in your toaster to transform ordinary white bread into browned, crispy toast? Two processes are going on in your toaster or broiler every time you turn it on to make toast. First, the heat made by the toaster/broiler dries out any moisture on the surface of the bread, which creates a dry, crispy crust. Then, the brown color of the crust develops as the sugars and starches in the bread undergo chemical changes. If you have ever heated sugar in a pan, you've seen that it turns brown when it gets hot. Do the following experiment to learn more about browning.

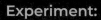
Which Toasts Better?

Purpose: *To understand the process of browning.*

Materials

2 slices of bread

2 teaspoons butter or vegetable oil spread

broiler pan

Procedure

1. Preheat the broiler. (Don't do this experiment in a toaster—you'll ruin the toaster!)

2. Spread the butter (or vegetable oil spread) on one slice of bread. Leave the other slice plain. Place both slices on a broiler pan.

3. Place the bread about 3–4 inches from the broiler and broil until one slice is nicely browned. Using pot holders, remove the pan from the broiler.

Observations

Record the answers to these questions in your *Science Chef Notebook* (see "About This Book" for how to set up your own notebook).

1. Compare the color of the two slices of bread and how much each was toasted.

2. Which slice of bread toasted more? Why do you think it toasted more?

The Science of Browning

When bread is exposed to heat, the surface dries and a crust forms. The crust browns because there is a chemical reaction between the protein and sugar in the bread when exposed to the heat. This browning action, called the **Maillard reaction**, causes new flavors and aromas. The Maillard reaction occurs in other foods as well, such as roasting vegetables or grilling meat.

Toasting means more than just toasting English muffins in your toaster. Toasting also refers to other foods browning and crisping when exposed to heat. The recipes in this chapter use different pieces of equipment for toasting, including a toaster, a broiler, and a frying pan.

What Happened in the Experiment?

When bread has butter or other spread on it, you won't get the browning action because the butter/spread keeps the bread from drying and forming a crust. The butter may brown a little but the bread itself won't brown or toast because it never formed a dry crust.

Awesome Avocado Toast

If you like avocado, here's a way to use one to make a quick and delicious breakfast or snack.

Difficulty: Intermediate / **Time:** 15–20 minutes to prepare / **Makes:** 1 serving

Ingredients

1 small avocado

½ teaspoon lemon juice

Salt, pinch

4 cherry tomatoes, sliced

1 slice whole-wheat or multi-grain bread

Avocado is the only fruit that ripens only after it is picked.

Avocados are ripe when soft to the touch (not mushy!).

Steps

1. Cut avocado in half lengthwise and remove the pit.

2. Scoop one half of the avocado into a small bowl and mash with a fork.

3. Add lemon juice and salt and continue mashing.

4. Carefully scoop the other half of the avocado away from the skin.

5. On a cutting board with a paring knife, slice the avocado into 5 or 6 slices. Slice each cherry tomato into at least two slices.

6. Toast the bread in a toaster.

7. Spread the mashed avocado on the top of the toast. Cut in half. Garnish with cherry tomatoes. Use the remaining avocado slices as a garnish on the plate.

High Tea Cinnamon Toast

This is a great recipe to share with a grandparent.

Difficulty: Intermediate / **Time:** 10 minutes / **Makes:** 2 servings

Steps

1. Preheat the broiler.

2. Mix together the sugar and cinnamon in a small bowl.

3. Place the bread on the broiler pan. Put the pan 6 inches from the broiler. Toast until golden brown and remove pan.

4. Turn the bread over and spread 1 teaspoon of butter or vegetable oil spread on each slice.

5. Sprinkle the sugar mixture evenly over the toast.

6. Place the bread back under the broiler with the sugar mixture facing up, and remove when sugar turns golden brown.

Ingredients

4 tablespoons sugar

1½ teaspoons cinnamon

4 slices whole-grain bread

4 teaspoons butter or vegetable oil spread

Using whole-grain bread provides more fiber and other nutrients than white bread.

Peanut Butter and Jelly French Toast Cutouts

This is a tasty recipe for breakfast, lunch, or a snack.

Difficulty: Beginner / **Time:** 15 minutes / **Makes:** 4 servings

Ingredients

4 tablespoons peanut butter

4 tablespoons jelly or jam

8 slices whole-grain bread

1 cup low-fat milk

1 egg, beaten with fork

1 teaspoon vanilla extract

2 tablespoons orange juice

½ teaspoon cinnamon

vegetable oil cooking spray

4 teaspoons confectioners' sugar

1 cup fresh chopped fruit or ½ cup maple syrup

For an eggless recipe, substitute 2 tablespoons of cornstarch for the egg and increase the milk to 1½ cups whole milk.

Steps

1. Spread peanut butter and jelly on 4 slices of bread. Lay the other 4 slices of bread on top, making 4 sandwiches.

2. Using your favorite cookie cutters, cut out shapes from your sandwiches.

3. Whisk the milk, egg, vanilla extract, orange juice, and cinnamon in the bowl.

4. Spray a frying pan with vegetable oil cooking spray. Put the frying pan on a burner set at medium-high and preheat for 2 minutes.

5. With a fork, dip the sandwich shapes in the egg mixture and place in the pan. When golden brown, turn the shapes over with a spatula, cooking the other side to finish.

6. Dust each cutout with 1 teaspoon confectioners' sugar and serve with fresh chopped fruit or maple syrup.

Variation

Cream-Cheese-and-Jelly French Toast Cutouts: Substitute 4 oz low-fat cream cheese (softened) for the peanut butter.

Linzer Tart French Toast

Linzer tarts are cookie sandwiches filled with raspberry jam. This recipe uses French toast instead of cookies. Make it on Valentine's Day and use a heart-shaped cookie cutter.

Difficulty: Intermediate / **Time:** 20 minutes / **Makes:** 4 servings

Ingredients

1½ cups low-fat milk

1 egg, beaten

2 tablespoons orange juice

1 teaspoon vanilla extract

½ teaspoon cinnamon

¼ teaspoon nutmeg

¼ teaspoon ground cloves

vegetable oil cooking spray

8 slices whole-grain bread

4 tablespoons raspberry jam

4 teaspoons confectioners' sugar

½ cup maple syrup (optional)

Steps

1. Mix the milk, egg, orange juice, vanilla extract, cinnamon, nutmeg, and cloves together in the bowl.

2. Spray a frying pan with vegetable oil cooking spray. Place the frying pan on a burner and preheat on medium-high for 2 minutes.

3. Dip each slice of bread into the egg mixture and place it in the pan. When each slice is golden brown underneath, turn it over and cook the other side.

4. Move each slice to a cutting board with a spatula and allow to cool slightly.

5. With the cookie cutter, cut a shape in the center of each of 4 slices of bread. Dust each shape lightly with confectioners' sugar.

6. Spread the remaining 4 slices of bread with raspberry jam.

7. Assemble by placing a shaped slice on top of each slice spread with jam. Dust 1 teaspoon confectioner's sugar on each and use maple syrup if you like.

Strawberry Butter

Try this delicious fruit spread on toast, biscuits, bagels, croissants, or pancakes. Take your pick!

Difficulty: Beginner / **Time:** 15 minutes / **Makes:** 12 servings (2 tablespoons each)

Ingredients

½ cup fresh strawberries

1 cup (2 sticks) unsalted butter, room temperature

¼ cup confectioners' sugar

Steps

1. Wash the strawberries in a colander and pat dry. Remove the leafy green top of each strawberry and the pale flesh right underneath it. Then use a cutting board and paring knife to cut each strawberry in half. Chop the berries.

2. Put the butter and sugar in a bowl. Use an electric mixer to beat until light and fluffy.

3. Fold in the strawberries with a rubber spatula.

4. Transfer into small serving dishes and refrigerate until ready to serve.

Unlike this recipe, apple butter is just applesauce that has been cooked for a long time so it is quite thick and brown in color.

Creamy Herb and Chive Spread

This is a tasty spread that's great on crackers for an afternoon snack.

Difficulty: Beginner / **Time:** 15 minutes +60 minutes for cream cheese to soften / **Makes:** 12 servings (2 tablespoons each)

Steps

1. Wash parsley and chives and pat dry with paper towels.

2. On a cutting board, use a knife to mince parsley and chives. Set aside.

3. On a cutting board, use a knife to cut the cream cheese into small cubes. Set aside for 1 hour.

4. Put cubes into the bowl and mash them by flattening them against the sides of the bowl with the wooden spoon.

5. Add chives and parsley to the bowl. Mix it thoroughly with the cheese. Serve with crackers or spread on toast.

Variation

Using grape tomatoes, or mini red or green peppers, remove the seeds to form a small bowl. Then fill the vegetables with the herb and chive spread. Bake in the oven at 350 °F (180 °C) for 15–18 minutes. Serve as an appetizer.

Ingredients

1 cup flat-leaf Italian parsley

½ cup fresh chives

1 (8½ oz) package cream cheese

> Many spreads and dips use herbs and spices mixed into a high-fat ingredient such as cream cheese or sour cream.

Ralph's Zippy Hummus

Hummus comes from the Middle East. Its main ingredient is chickpeas, a sweet and nutty food that becomes creamy when blended. This homemade version makes a delicious spread for pita chips or raw vegetables.

Difficulty: Intermediate / **Time:** 25–30 minutes / **Makes:** 24 2-tablespoon servings

Ingredients

3 garlic cloves

2 15-oz cans chickpeas

1 roasted red pepper (canned or bottled is fine)

½ cup olive oil

½ cup tahini

3 tablespoons lemon juice

1½ tablespoons chili powder

1½ tablespoons cumin

1 tablespoon paprika

¼ teaspoon salt

⅛ teaspoon cayenne pepper

1 cucumber

crackers or flatbread (optional)

Steps

1. Place the garlic cloves into a jar with a lid (or a metal pot with a lid). Shake the garlic vigorously for 15–30 seconds, or until you open the lid and find the garlic cloves have separated from their peels.

2. Place remaining ingredients (except the cucumber) in a food processor. Blend for 5 minutes.

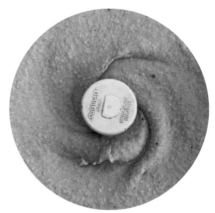

3. Place the hummus in the refrigerator to chill for 15 minutes.

4. While it chills, wash the cucumber. Using a cutting board and paring knife, slice the cucumber into ½-inch slices.

5. You are going to use a pastry bag to pipe the hummus onto the cucumbers. First you need to put a piping tip down in the bottom of the pastry bag. To fill the pastry bag, hold it in the middle and fold the top half down over your hand. Then use a spatula or spoon to scoop the filling into the bottom of the bag. Fill the bag only a little more than half full.

6. Twist the top of the bag and put pressure on it to pipe the hummus onto the cucumber slices, crackers, or flatbread.

If you don't have a pastry bag, use a plastic sandwich bag and snip off one bottom corner.

Tahini is made of toasted sesame seeds that have been ground to create a paste that is lighter in color and not as thick as peanut butter.

Video at http:// www.wiley .com/go/ sciencechef.

Chapter 5

How Does a Bean Sprout?

~~~~~~

Most plants and trees produce flowers. Once flowers bloom, they work on making seeds from which new plants and trees will grow. A **seed** contains a tiny plant that will start to grow in soil when given enough water and warmth. But seeds will be produced only if the flower is pollinated. **Pollen** is a powdery yellowish grain made by the flower. **Pollination** is when pollen is transferred between parts of the flower (often by bees), which then allows the flower to produce a seed. For example, an apple tree produces flowers in the spring. After the bees or another insect pollinates the flowers, the flowers start to grow apples. Inside of each apple are many seeds that can be planted to grow more apple trees.

Beans are the seeds found in a special group of flowering plants. You have probably eaten beans in dishes such as baked beans, burritos, or bean soup. Beans come in a variety of colors and are usually less than 1 inch in length. Popular beans include dark red kidney beans, black beans, and pinto beans.

Beans grow in a protected structure called a **pod** that hangs down from the bean plant. The photo here shows you three pods and also three soybeans from one of the pods. One pod has been cut open to reveal where the beans grew. Each bean has a protective **seed coat** on the outside. On the inside is an **embryo** that develops into a new plant, including the roots, leaves, and stem, under the right conditions. The experiment will help you see how a small bean becomes a new plant.

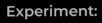
Which Beans Will Start to Grow?

Purpose: *To find out how water affects whether a bean will sprout.*

Materials

18 dry beans

medium bowl

2 plates or cookie sheets

paper towels

Procedure

1. Before the dry beans can be used in this experiment, they must be soaked in water overnight. Place the beans in a medium bowl and fill with 3 inches of cold water. Let stand overnight at room temperature.

2. In the morning, drain the beans.

3. Place half the beans on a dry paper towel on a plate or cookie sheet. This is group A.

4. Dampen a paper towel and lay on a plate or cookie sheet. Place the remaining beans on top of the paper towel. Spray water on the beans. This is group B.

5. Place both plates or cookie sheets close to each other for several days in a bright area, but not in direct sunlight. Spray water only on group B three to four times daily.

Observations

Record the answers to these questions in your *Science Chef Notebook* (see "About This Book" for how to set up your own notebook).

1. Which group of beans sprouts first?

2. Why did this group sprout first?

From Seed to Plant

If beans find their way into soil, the embryo inside will start to grow (also called **sprouting** or **germination**) when given enough water, nutrients, and warmth, as shown in the drawing. The bean first pushes out roots into the soil. The roots will bring water and nutrients from the soil to the plant. Next, a stem with two leaves from the seed pushes up through the soil into the sunshine. The leaves contain stored food but will soon be making their own food. Germination ends when the leaves push through the soil to the sunlight. The plant needs water, nutrients found in the soil, warmth, and sunlight to continue to grow.

What Happened in the Experiment?

The beans that were kept moist (group B) are the ones that sprout within a week. The first structure that grows out of each bean is the root of the new plant. To sprout, beans need warmth and moisture. The beans in both groups had the same warmth, but the beans in group A didn't have enough water to sprout. Now, you can transfer the sprouted beans to soil so they continue to grow.

Southwestern Dinner Salad

On a hot summer day, try this cold and tasty dinner salad.

Difficulty: Intermediate / **Time:** 20–25 minutes / **Makes:** 4 entrée servings

Ingredients

14-oz can black beans

6 cups mixed greens

½ cucumber

½ red pepper

½ yellow pepper

1 ripe avocado

1 small red onion
(½ cup chopped)

1 cup canned diced
tomatoes, drained

1 cup bean sprouts or
broccoli sprouts

¾ cup corn

2 teaspoons lemon juice

1 teaspoon cumin

¼ teaspoon salt

¼ teaspoon pepper

½ cup prepared or home-
made Italian salad dressing

Steps

1. Drain the black beans. Put the beans into a colander and rinse. Set the beans aside.

2. Wash all the vegetables and pat dry.

3. Peel the cucumber. On a cutting board, cut the cucumber into slices and then dice.

4. Remove the seeds from the peppers. Cut the peppers into ½-inch strips. Cut the strips into small pieces.

5. Cut the avocado in half. Take out the pit. Take the avocado flesh out of the skin. Slice into ¼-inch slices. Carefully toss the avocado with lemon juice in a small bowl and cover with plastic wrap until ready to use.

6. Remove the outer skin from the onion. On a cutting board, cut the onion in half and chop.

7. Place the cumin, salt, pepper, black beans, cucumber, peppers, avocado, onion, and remaining ingredients (except dressing) in a large bowl.

8. Lightly toss with salad dressing and serve.

South-western food is found in Arizona, New Mexico, and parts of Colorado and Utah. It has been influenced by Spanish, Mexican, and Native American cultures.

"Aquafabulous" Cornbread

If you want to make cornbread without any animal ingredients, it turns out that the liquid in a can of chickpeas (which is called **aquafaba**) is very useful because it whips and traps air. To make this cornbread, aquafaba is whipped just like egg whites, which gives cornbread a taller and fluffier texture.

Difficulty: Intermediate / **Time:** 30 minutes to prepare +30–35 minutes to bake / **Makes:** 16 squares

Ingredients

¼ cup olive oil plus flour to dust pan

1 cup all-purpose flour

1 cup cornmeal

1½ teaspoons baking powder

½ teaspoon baking soda

¼ teaspoon salt

¾ cup unsweetened almond milk

1 teaspoon lemon juice

½ cup chickpea brine (drain a 15-oz can of chickpeas)

2/3 cup sugar

¼ teaspoon cream of tartar

Steps

1. Preheat the oven to 350 °F (180 °C).

2. Lightly brush an 8-inch square baking pan with olive oil and then lightly dust with flour. Shake off any excess flour.

3. In a large bowl, stir together the flour, cornmeal, baking powder, baking soda, and salt. Set aside.

4. In a small bowl, combine the almond milk and lemon juice and let sit until it looks bubbly.

5. Add the chickpea brine to a medium bowl. With a handheld electric, or tabletop mixer, beat the chickpea brine until foamy. Slowly add the sugar and cream of tartar and beat until soft peaks form. The brine should be shiny and moist. This takes about 5 minutes.

6. Add the milk and lemon juice to the flour mixture and combine.

7. Add the aquafaba mixture in three parts, gently folding (over-and-under motion) into the batter. Repeat until batter is smooth and all ingredients are thoroughly incorporated. Do not overmix. Pour batter into the pan.

8. Bake for 30–35 minutes at 350°F (180°C) until the edges are golden brown and a toothpick comes out completely clean when inserted in the middle of the bread. Let cool for 15 minutes before cutting into 2-inch squares.

Aquafaba from canned chickpeas can also substitute for whole eggs in baking recipes. To replace one egg, use 3 tablespoons aquafaba.

Video at http://www.wiley.com/go/sciencechef.

Santa Fe Cheesy Black Bean Soup

This is a hearty, healthy soup for the fall and winter months.

Difficulty: Intermediate / **Time:** 70 minutes / **Makes:** 12 cups

Ingredients

1 medium onion
(1 cup chopped)

½ green pepper

1 tablespoon olive oil

1 teaspoon garlic powder

1 teaspoon dried oregano

4 (15-oz) cans undrained,
cooked black beans

2 (14-oz) cans undrained
diced tomatoes

4 cups vegetable broth

2 tablespoons lemon juice

1 tablespoon cumin

½ teaspoon salt

¼ teaspoon cayenne pepper

1 cup shredded
cheddar cheese

Steps

1. Remove the outer skin from the onion. Using a paring knife on a cutting board, cut the onion in half and chop.

2. Cut the peppers into ½-in. strips (remove the seeds). Cut the strips into small pieces.

3. Preheat a large Dutch oven for about 2 minutes on medium heat. Add the olive oil and let heat up. Add the onion, pepper, garlic powder, and oregano and sauté for about 5 minutes.

4. Add the beans, tomatoes, vegetable broth, lemon juice, cumin, salt, and cayenne pepper to the pot and stir. Bring to a boil for 1 minute.

5. Turn the heat to low and cover. Simmer the soup for 30 minutes.

6. Turn off the heat and uncover. Let the soup stand for about 10 minutes.

7. Measure six cups of soup and place in food processor. Process all ingredients until thick and creamy.

8. Add the blended soup back to the pot and turn the heat to medium. Cook the soup for an additional 10 minutes.

9. Ladle the soup into soup crocks or bowls. Top with cheddar cheese and serve immediately.

Santa Fe is the capital city of New Mexico and home to southwestern cooking using lots of beans and tomatoes.

Quick-and-Easy Lunchtime Burrito

Burrito means "little donkey" and is a popular Mexican-American food. Whereas burritos are big enough for a meal and rolled up in a wheat flour tortilla, tacos are more snack size and use a corn tortilla that is folded in half.

Difficulty: Intermediate / **Time:** 25–30 minutes / **Makes:** 6 burritos

Ingredients

6 burrito-size flour tortillas

1 small onion (½ cup chopped)

1 tablespoon oil

1 pound ground beef, chicken, or turkey

¼ teaspoon ground cumin

¼ teaspoon chili powder

10-oz can enchilada sauce

14-oz can refried beans

½ cup grated cheddar cheese

Steps

1. Preheat the oven to 250°F (120°C).

2. Wrap the tortillas in aluminum foil and place in the oven to heat up.

3. Remove the outer skin from the onion. Using a paring knife on a cutting board, cut the onion in half and chop.

4. Add oil to a frying pan and preheat the pan for about 2 minutes on medium heat. Cook the onion until softened. Then add the ground meat and cook until it is cooked through.

5. Add the cumin, chili powder, and most (not all) of the enchilada sauce.

6. Simmer the meat mixture over low heat for 5 more minutes.

7. Meanwhile heat the refried beans in a small saucepan over medium heat for 5 minutes.

8. Remove the tortillas from the oven. Using the first tortilla, add a small amount of beans, then a small amount of meat and some grated cheese.

9. As shown in the photo, first fold in the sides, then roll up from the bottom. Repeat with the rest of the tortillas and place the burritos into a baking dish. Drizzle the remaining enchilada sauce on the tortillas and cover with aluminum foil.

10. Return the burritos to the oven for 5 min, then serve.

Refried beans are cooked in water and fried once with fat and finally mashed until no whole beans remain.

Enchilada sauce is made from chile peppers, tomatoes, onion, garlic, and traditional Mexican spices such as cumin.

Chapter 6

How Do Sauces Thicken?

Although few people bother making their own sauces, homemade sauce is worth the extra effort. A sauce is any flavorful liquid (usually thickened) that is served on other foods, like ketchup on French fries. Many sauces need to be thickened so they are the right consistency to pour over foods such as chicken, pasta, or vegetables.

Foods containing a lot of starch (such as flour) are often used as thickeners in cooking. When heated in liquid, a starch undergoes a process called **gelatinization**. When starches gelatinize, the starch granules absorb water and swell, making the liquid thicken. Around the boiling point, the granules have absorbed so much water that they burst and starch pours out into the liquid. When this occurs, the liquid quickly becomes still thicker. See how flour thickens in this experiment.

Which Is the Better Thickener?

Purpose: *To understand how flour thickens.*

Procedure

1. Put 2 cups of broth into a small saucepan on medium heat. Heat on medium for 5 minutes or until hot. Add 2 tablespoons of flour to the broth, using the whip to stir. Turn the heat up a little and stir for a few more minutes. Turn off the heat and observe how the broth has changed.

2. Put 2 cups of broth into a medium saucepan and heat on medium for 5 minutes or until hot.

3. Meanwhile, place ¼ cup *cold* water and 2 tablespoons flour into a small bowl and thoroughly mix the water with the flour using a wire whip. Make sure there are no lumps.

4. Once the broth is hot, slowly add the combined flour and water into the broth, whipping constantly. Turn the heat up a little and stir the broth until it is thick and bubbly. Turn off the heat and observe how the broth has changed.

Materials

32 oz carton beef, chicken, or vegetable broth or stock

4 tablespoons all-purpose flour, divided

small bowl

whip

wooden spoon

medium saucepan

Thicken stock with flour. | Thicken stock with flour and water.

Observations

Record the answers to these questions in your *Science Chef Notebook* (see "About This Book" for how to set up your own notebook).

1. What did the broth look like in each pan at the end once the heat was turned off?

2. Rate the degree of thickening that occurred in the pan when the broth was thickened with flour. Rate from 1 (consistency of water) to 5 (consistency of a thick milkshake).

3. Rate the degree of thickening that occurred in the pan when the broth was thickened with flour mixed with water. Rate from 1 (consistency of water) to 5 (consistency of a thick milkshake).

All About Thickeners

The thickener called **roux** is a mixture of flour and fat cooked together. The fat (usually butter) is melted in a pan, and then the flour is added and stirred until the mixture is smooth. The roux is then added to sauces, soups, and gravies to thicken and create a creamy texture. The starch in the flour gelatinizes, which causes the thickening. Cooking the flour and fat first helps remove the raw flour flavor and also coats the flour particles with fat so you don't get lumps in your sauce, soup, or gravy.

Another good thickener is cornstarch, which is made from corn and has to be mixed first with water (like flour) before adding it to a hot liquid to prevent lumps. Unlike flour, cornstarch is gluten free. Starchy foods, such as rice and potatoes, also help thicken soups and other dishes.

Flour   Cornstarch   Rice

What Happened in This Experiment?

When you added flour directly to the broth, you saw lumps develop. The broth heated with the flour and water mixture thickened better and had no lumps. By whipping the flour in cold water first, the starch granules are kept separated so they're less likely to link together and form clumps when they meet the hot liquid. Then the starch can gelatinize properly and do its job creating the desired thickening. (You would have had the same results if you had used cornstarch and water instead of flour and water.)

Over-the-Rainbow Mac and Cheese

In this recipe, you make a cheese sauce from roux, milk, and cheese. The cheese sauce is served over hot pasta. Pasta is a general term for any shape of noodles, such as spaghetti or elbow macaroni.

Difficulty: Intermediate / **Time:** 35 minutes / **Makes:** 8 servings

Ingredients

4 quarts water

1½ cups spinach leaves

12 oz tricolor rotini pasta

2 tablespoons butter or vegetable oil spread

2 tablespoons flour

1¼ cups low-fat (2%) milk

8 oz shredded cheddar cheese

1 tablespoon Dijon mustard

½ teaspoon salt

¼ teaspoon nutmeg

¼ teaspoon paprika

⅛ teaspoon cayenne pepper

Steps

1. In a large saucepan, bring the water to a boil.

2. While waiting for the water to boil, rinse the spinach and pat dry. Place the spinach leaves on a small cutting board and cut off the stems. Set the spinach aside.

3. Once the water is boiling, carefully add the rotini pasta. Cook the pasta for about 10 minutes until al dente—meaning not too firm but not too soft, either.

4. Place a colander in the sink and drain the pasta. Transfer pasta to a large bowl. Toss the spinach leaves in the pasta.

5. Melt the butter or vegetable oil spread in a medium saucepan over low heat. Cook until a little bubbly.

6. Add the flour to the saucepan and cook for 3–4 minutes over low heat, stirring frequently with a wooden spoon. Do not let it brown.

7. Slowly add the milk to the flour mixture, stirring constantly until all the milk has been added. Heat the milk mixture on medium heat and continue stirring until the milk almost reaches a boil.

8. Add the cheese, mustard, and remaining ingredients to the saucepan and cook until the cheese melts. Pour the cheese sauce over the pasta and spinach and serve.

Adding pasta to boiling water and removing the pasta (once cooked) needs to be done carefully to avoid burns.

In the early stages of cooking, the starch in pasta gets sticky so stirring the pasta at this time will prevent it from sticking together.

Video at http://www.wiley.com/go/sciencechef.

Chile Con Queso Dip

Chile con queso is a thick sauce of melted cheese seasoned with chile peppers, typically served warm as a dip for tortilla chips. You will use cornstarch for thickening this dip just right.

Difficulty: Beginner / **Time:** 25 minutes / **Makes:** 24 servings

Ingredients

1 medium onion
(1 cup chopped)

2 tablespoons butter or
vegetable oil

4-oz can chopped
green chiles

2 tablespoons cornstarch

1 cup low-fat (2%) milk

2 cups shredded Monterey
Jack cheese

2 cups shredded
cheddar cheese

½ cup low-fat sour cream

Salt (to taste)

Tortilla chips, 13 oz bag

Steps

1. Remove the outer, papery skin from the onion. On a cutting board, use a knife to cut the onion in half. Lay each onion half flat on the cutting board and chop into small pieces.

2. Preheat a saucepan by placing on a burner set to medium heat for 2 minutes. Add butter or oil to the pan. Add the onions and sauté for about 5 minutes until almost tender. Add the chilies and cook and stir for 5 more minutes.

3. In a small bowl, mix the cornstarch and milk with a whip until smooth. Stir into the onion mixture.

4. Bring to a boil. Cook and stir about 1–2 minutes or until thickened.

5. Reduce heat to low. Add shredded cheeses in slowly and in small amounts, allowing the cheese to melt in between additions.

6. Stir in sour cream and salt to taste. Remove from heat.

7. Serve warm with tortilla chips, or any type of chips, crackers, flatbread, or toasted pita bread, as well as vegetables such as celery or cherry tomatoes.

There are many types of chiles, also known as chile peppers, and some are known for being *very hot*! Monterey Jack cheese is a top choice for melting.

Chapter 7

How Does Bread Rise?

~~~~~~~~~~~~~~~~~~~~~~~~~~~~~~~

Yeast breads are one of the world's favorite foods. Breads go with virtually any meal. They're also very simple, using just a few ingredients: mainly flour, water, sugar, and yeast. **Yeast** is a helpful fungus made of just one cell that makes bread dough rise (expand). Yeast feeds on the sugar for energy and releases carbon dioxide gas as a result. Carbon dioxide gas gets trapped in the dough and makes it rise. When the dough is cooked, the trapped gas leaves the little holes you see in bread that give it its soft texture. Learn more about yeast in the following experiment.

How Does Sugar Affect Yeast's Growth?

Purpose: *To compare the growth of yeast with and without sugar.*

Procedure

1. With a magic marker, label one bottle with "A" and the other with "B."

2. Fill up each bottle between half and two thirds full with warm (not hot) water. Use a thermometer and make sure the water is between 105 and 115°F (40–46°C).

3. Add 1 teaspoon of yeast to each bottle and shake each bottle a little.

4. Add 2 teaspoons of sugar to the bottle labeled "A" and swish the sugar around.

5. Place a deflated balloon over each bottle. Leave for 1 hour, checking every 15 minutes.

Materials

2 empty bottles (20 fl. oz to 1 quart in size)

warm water

1 packet active dry yeast

2 teaspoons sugar

Yeast and sugar in A.

A

B

Only yeast in B.

Observations

Record the answers to these questions in your *Science Chef Notebook* (see "About This Book" for how to set up your own notebook).

1. Which balloon(s) becomes inflated with the most carbon dioxide gas?

2. What contributed to the balloon(s) becoming inflated?

Steps to Make Bread

This chapter includes some recipes for bread dough, but first you need to know some basic rules about growing yeast and the steps to make bread.

Proofing the Yeast

The first step in using yeast is proofing, which means dissolving the yeast in warm liquid, usually water. You have to take care not to kill the yeast by using water that is too hot. Yeast grows best in liquid that is between 105 and 115 °F (40–46 °C). If the water is too cold, it will take longer for the yeast to grow, and the bread will not rise as much. If you do not have a thermometer to check the exact temperature, put some water on your wrist and make sure it feels warm, not hot.

Mixing the Dough

After you've started the yeast growing in warm water, add your ingredients and stir them into a ball of dough. The dough should be a little sticky but not so sticky that you can't get it off your fingers. When a dough is too sticky, you need to add a little more flour.

Kneading the Dough

Once the dough is just right, place it on a lightly floured board for kneading. **Kneading** is the process of working dough into a smooth mass by pressing and folding. This mixes the ingredients and develops the gluten. **Gluten**, a protein, is created when wheat flour is mixed with water. Gluten is important because it is elastic and can inflate with carbon dioxide gas (like a balloon) as the dough rises and then bakes in the oven. Kneading is important for the bread to have the right texture. To knead, follow these steps:

1. Lift the edge of the dough farthest from you and fold the dough in half toward you.

2. Press the dough down and away from you with the heel of your hand.

3. Turn the dough a quarter turn.

4. Continue folding, pressing, and turning until the dough feels smooth and elastic. If the dough feels sticky, add a sprinkling of flour.

How to Knead Dough

Fold the dough toward you.

Push the dough away with the heel of your hand.

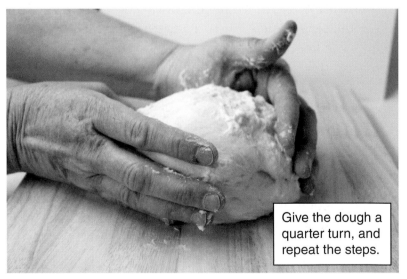

Give the dough a quarter turn, and repeat the steps.

Letting the Dough Rise

After the dough is kneaded, place it in a lightly greased bowl, cover the bowl with a clean, damp towel, and put the bowl in a warm, draft-free area. Let the dough rest and rise until double in size. As the dough rises, the yeast eats the sugars and makes carbon dioxide gas.

Punching the Dough

When the dough has risen (usually it takes about 1–1½ hours for bread), test it by inserting your fingers in the dough to the first knuckle in several places. If the finger marks close very slowly, the dough is ready to be punched—which does not mean that you hit the dough with your fist! To punch the dough, pull it up on all sides, fold over the center, and press down. Punching keeps the dough at an even temperature, removes the gas, further develops the gluten, and brings fresh oxygen to the yeast cells so they make more gas.

Shaping the Dough

Once the dough is punched, divide it (if necessary), shape into desired shapes (rolls, loaves), and place onto nonstick or lightly oiled sheet pans or other baking dishes. Let the dough rise again, until double in bulk. When poked with fingers, a fully risen loaf of dough will slowly fill out the dents made by the fingers. After the second rising, place directly into a preheated oven and bake until the bread is browned and sounds hollow when tapped.

To save time, you can buy frozen bread dough (usually in one-pound loaves) at the supermarket that, after thawing, is ready to rise and be baked. Some people also have bread machines that do all the work for you. But it's much more fun to do it by hand!

What Happened in the Experiment?

Without the sugar (Bottle "B"), the yeast has nothing to eat and can't inflate a balloon. Meanwhile in Bottle "A," the yeast has been munching on the sugar and producing enough gas to inflate the balloon.

All-American White Bread

Difficulty: Intermediate / **Time:** 4½ hours / **Makes:** 1 loaf, 16 slices

Ingredients

½ cup warm water at 105–115°F (40–46°C)

1 package active dry yeast

1 teaspoon sugar

¾ cup low-fat (2%) milk

2 tablespoons sugar

2 tablespoons melted butter or vegetable oil spread

1 teaspoon salt

2¾–3 cups bread flour

> When two proteins in flour are moistened with water, they combine to make the large protein called gluten. Gluten makes the bread dough elastic and also helps give bread its texture.
>
> Bread flour is higher in protein than regular all-purpose flour.

Steps

1. Put water in a medium bowl. Using a thermometer, make sure the water is between 105 and 115°F (40–46°C) so you don't kill or chill the yeast.

2. Add the yeast and teaspoon of sugar to the water and stir well. Let rest for 10 minutes.

3. Place the milk in a measuring cup and microwave on high for 30 seconds or until the milk is warm, about 85°F (30°C).

4. In a large bowl, whisk the milk, sugar, melted butter or vegetable oil spread, and salt together until creamy. Add half of the flour and stir with a wooden spoon until smooth.

5. Add the yeast mixture and just enough of the remaining flour until the mixture forms a ball.

6. Knead the dough on a lightly floured surface for 8–10 minutes. Fold the dough in half toward you. Then press the dough down and away from you with the heel of your hand. Give the dough a quarter turn, then return to folding the dough in half.

7. Continue folding, pressing, and turning until the dough feels smooth and elastic. While kneading, add just enough flour so the dough is not sticking in clumps to the board or your hands.

8. Form the dough into a ball and place it in a medium bowl that you have lightly coated with vegetable oil. Turn the dough over in the bowl so the dough has a thin layer of oil on it.

9. Cover the bowl with a damp towel or plastic wrap and place the bowl in a warm place to rise until the dough doubles in size – about 60 to 90 minutes.

10. When you can poke your finger in the dough and it closes back slowly, it is time to punch down the dough.

11. Lightly grease a 9 × 5-inch loaf pan with vegetable oil spread. On a lightly floured surface, roll the dough into a rectangle, about 7 × 9 inches. Roll the dough from the shorter end and place seam side down in the loaf pan. Cover the bread with another damp towel and let rise for about 30 minutes.

12. Preheat the oven to 375 °F (190 °C).

13. Bake at 375 °F (190 °C) for 35–40 minutes or until bread is golden brown and sounds hollow when tapped. Place on cooling rack until cooled. Serve at your favorite picnic,

Basic Pizza Dough

Pizza dough is made like bread dough but doesn't have to rise, so it is ready to use in just 25 minutes.

Difficulty: Intermediate / **Time:** 20–25 minutes / **Makes:** 1 ball of pizza dough (enough for a 12-inch pizza with 8 slices)

Ingredients

1 cup warm water

1 package active dry yeast

1 teaspoon sugar

1 teaspoon salt

2 tablespoons oil

2–3 cups all-purpose or whole-wheat flour

Unlike bread, pizza dough can be used right after being made. The heat of the oven will help the pizza crust rise up sufficiently.

Steps

1. Using a thermometer, make sure the water temperature is between 105 and 115°F (40–46°C) so you don't kill (or chill) the yeast.

2. Add the yeast to the water in a bowl and stir.

3. Add the sugar, salt, and oil to the water and stir well.

4. Add the flour to the bowl in small amounts and stir well after each addition. Add just enough flour so the dough is not sticking in clumps to your hands or the bowl.

5. Using your hands, knead dough for 2–3 minutes on a lightly floured surface.

6. Let the dough rest 5–10 minutes before using.

Possibilities Pizza

Use the Basic Pizza Dough recipe to make your own signature pizza.

Difficulty: Intermediate / **Time:** 45 minutes / **Makes:** 8 slices

Steps

1. Preheat oven to 425°F (220°C). If using a **pizza stone**, take out the top oven rack and place the stone on the middle rack. Preheat the pizza stone for 45 minutes.

2. Wash the vegetables and, using a knife, slice them on a cutting board.

3. Preheat a frying pan by placing it on a burner and setting heat to medium for 2 minutes. Add 1 tablespoon olive oil. Add the vegetables and sauté for 3 minutes.

4. Lightly sprinkle a rectangular baking sheet or pizza peel with cornmeal. Roll out the dough on the sheet or pizza peel to approximately a 9 × 13-inch rectangle.

5. Brush the pizza dough lightly with 2 teaspoons olive oil. Spread pizza sauce, then sautéed vegetables, shredded cheese, and olives (if desired) on the dough.

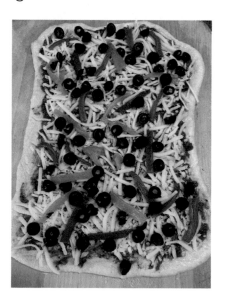

Ingredients

1 cup sliced vegetables such as mushrooms, green or red peppers, or onions

1 tablespoon olive oil

3 tablespoons cornmeal

1 recipe Basic Pizza Dough

2 teaspoons olive oil

1 jar (15½-oz) pizza sauce

6 oz shredded part-skim mozzarella cheese

¼ cup sliced olives (optional)

6. Bake the pizza at 425 °F (220 °C) for 20–25 minutes until the crust is lightly browned and the cheese is bubbly. If using a pizza stone, take the pizza off the pizza stone with the peel.

Home ovens lack the high heat needed at the start of baking to make the crust crispy without overcooking the toppings. When you put the pizza on a pizza stone, the crust starts to cook right away so you get a better crust and the pizza cooks more evenly.

Tip: Sautéing the vegetables helps develop their flavor and color.

"Saucy" Sausage and Veggie Stromboli

Stromboli has the same ingredients as pizza, only it is rolled up.

Difficulty: Intermediate / **Time:** 30 minutes to prepare +35–40 minutes to bake / **Makes:** 8 slices

Steps

1. Preheat oven to 375 °F (190 °C).

2. Preheat a frying pan. Add 1 tablespoon vegetable oil. Sauté the sausage links on medium heat for 10 minutes until golden brown. Let the sausage cool and slice into ¼-inch slices.

3. While the sausage cools, squeeze out any extra water in the spinach and pat dry with a paper towel.

4. Remove the outer skin from the onion. Using a knife on a cutting board, slice the onion in half, then cut the onion into slices. Wrap up the other half and refrigerate.

5. Preheat the frying pan again. Add 1 tablespoon oil. Add the onions and sauté for 3 minutes.

6. On a floured surface, pat the pizza dough into a rectangle measuring about 11 × 14 inches. Brush the dough lightly with 1 tablespoon of olive oil. Spread the sauce on the dough, leaving a ¼-inch border all around. Sprinkle on the cheese.

7. Lay the sausage slices on the cheese. Evenly spread the spinach and onion toppings on the dough.

8. Roll up the dough lengthwise like a jelly roll, and close the ends tightly.

Ingredients

2 links medium Italian sausage

3 tablespoons vegetable oil, divided

½ cup chopped frozen spinach, thawed

½ medium onion (½ cup chopped)

1 recipe Basic Pizza Dough

½ cup pizza sauce

4 oz mozzarella cheese, grated

vegetable oil cooking spray

2 teaspoons olive oil

9. Spray a cookie sheet with cooking spray and place the stromboli on the sheet.

10. Cut three slits in the top of the stromboli for steam to escape. Brush lightly with the 2 teaspoons of olive oil. Bake stromboli at 375 °F (190 °C) for 35–40 minutes or until golden brown.

Sautéing the onion brings out the flavor of the natural sugars in the onion.

Brushing the stromboli with oil before baking prevents the crust from drying out.

11. Remove from oven. Allow to cool 5 minutes, then cut into eight slices and serve.

Monkey Bread

Monkey Bread is fun to make and is pulled apart to be eaten.

Difficulty: Intermediate / **Time:** 25 minutes to prepare, 30 minutes to rise, and 60 minutes to bake / **Makes:** 15 servings

Steps

1. Grease a 10-inch tube cake pan with shortening.

2. Pack the light brown sugar into a measuring cup. Combine the brown sugar, white sugar, and cinnamon in a small bowl. Mix well.

3. With flour-dusted hands, tear off 1½-inch pieces of dough. Roll each piece into a ball.

4. Dip each dough ball into the melted vegetable oil spread, then roll in the cinnamon-sugar mixture until completely coated.

5. Place each ball in the tube pan.

6. Continue to coat the balls and place in the pan about ½ inch apart, building up layers until the dough is used or the pan is about three quarters full.

Ingredients

1 tablespoon shortening

1 cup light brown sugar

¾ cup white sugar

1 teaspoon cinnamon flour for dusting

3 loaves frozen bread dough (allow to thaw and rise according to instructions on package)

OR 1½ recipe White Bread dough

¾ cup vegetable oil spread, melted

A tube pan is a deep, smooth-sided baking pan with a hollow tube in the middle. It is used for making angel food cake and sponge cakes.

Video at http://www.wiley.com/go/sciencechef.

7. Cover the pan with a clean, damp kitchen towel and let stand in a warm place until the dough rises to the top of the pan, about 30 minutes.

8. Preheat the oven to 350 °F (180 °C). Put the pan in the oven and bake for 60 minutes, covering loosely with foil if the top begins to get too brown.

9. Remove the bread from the oven and let cool for 10 minutes.

10. Turn the bread pan upside down, holding one hand under the bread. Let the bread slip out of the pan.

11. Serve the bread warm. To eat, pull the loaf apart.

Chapter 8

What Is Baking Powder?

Take a teaspoon of baking powder and add it to a cup of water. What happens? The baking powder makes the water bubble. **Baking powder** contains baking soda (a base) and an acid. *Acids* are sour tasting chemical compounds and *bases* have a bitter taste. Acids and bases react together. In the presence of moisture or heat, baking soda reacts with an acid to produce carbon dioxide bubbles (the same you see in soft drinks and carbonated water). In baked goods, the bubbles swell the food being baked, resulting in, for example, cupcakes that rise during baking. Do the following experiment to learn more about how baking powder works.

Does Temperature Affect How Much Baking Powder Bubbles?

Purpose: *To show how temperature affects the actions of baking powder.*

Materials

2 teaspoons double-acting baking powder

2 1-cup glass measuring cups

small saucepan

Procedure

1. Put ¾ cup cold water in a 1-cup measuring cup. Likewise, put ¾ cup hot water in another 1-cup measuring cup.

2. Add 1 teaspoon of baking powder to each cup. Do not mix.

3. Observe the reaction in each cup.

4. When there are no more bubbles in the glass with the cold water, heat the water in a small pan on the stove over medium heat. Observe the reaction.

Observations

Record the answers to these questions in your *Science Chef Notebook* (see "About This Book" for how to set up your own notebook).

1. Did the cup with the cold water or the cup with the hot water have more bubbles?

2. What happened when you heated the cold water with baking powder on the stove?

Baking Powder and Quick Breads

Baking powder is used in most baking recipes that don't rely on yeast (see Chapter 7). Yeast is a live organism that is commonly used in making bread. It also produces carbon dioxide bubbles. Baking powder is used to make most cakes, cookies, biscuits, and quick breads.

Quick breads are just what the name implies— breads made quickly! This category includes muffins, pancakes, waffles, loaf breads such as banana bread, and biscuits. White bread and whole-wheat bread require yeast to make them rise (which takes a lot of time); quick breads use baking powder so they rise rapidly in the oven and are usually baked in an hour or less.

Making muffins is easy. Just pay attention to these baking tips.

- Once the batter is ready, put it into pans and bake right away. Baking powder starts its activity as soon as the batter is made, so it's important to get the muffins into the oven as soon as possible.

- Fill the muffin tins evenly and put a little water in any empty cups.

- Bake on the center rack so the bottoms do not burn and the muffins cook evenly.

- Bake until golden brown and a wooden toothpick inserted into the center comes out clean. Over-baked muffins are dry because too much moisture escaped as steam.

Use a toothpick to test for doneness.

Let muffins cool for 5 minutes before you remove them from the pan. Always use pot holders when you do this: simply turn the pan upside down over a cooling rack.

What Happened in the Experiment?

In this experiment, you saw that baking powder makes more carbon dioxide bubbles when mixed with hot rather than cold water. This is why the baking powder you use is called *double acting*. Double-acting baking powder reacts once when it is exposed to moisture (such as when you are mixing up a muffin batter that includes milk) and then *again* when exposed to the heat of the oven. Therefore, the presence of both moisture and heat in the hot water caused more of a reaction. When mixed in cold water, the baking powder did produce bubbles, and it also produced bubbles when heated on the stove. This is exactly the way baking powder is supposed to work: to produce some carbon dioxide when the batter is being mixed and then again when the batter is put into the oven.

Baking Powder Drop Biscuits

In colder months, serve warm with honey, apple butter, or jam. In warmer months, use these biscuits in the next recipe for Breakfast Strawberry Shortcakes.

Difficulty: Intermediate / **Time:** 35 minutes / **Makes:** 12 biscuits

Steps

1. Preheat oven to 400 °F (205 °C).

2. Combine the flour, baking powder, baking soda, and salt in a medium bowl.

3. Put the butter in the bowl. Holding a table knife in each hand, draw the knives across each other to cut through the butter and dry ingredients. Keep cutting until the flour and fat mixture is in pieces about the shape of peas.

4. Stir in the buttermilk just until the dry ingredients are moistened.

5. Knead the dough on a lightly floured surface five times. Knead by pressing it out, then folding it in half. After folding, give the dough a quarter turn and start again.

6. Pat the dough out to a ½-inch thickness. Cut out biscuits with a 2-inch round cutter (or use a juice glass).

7. Place biscuits 1 inch apart on an ungreased cookie sheet. Brush biscuits with melted butter or vegetable oil spread. Bake 12–14 minutes at 400 °F (205 °C) or until golden brown.

Ingredients

2 cups all-purpose flour

1 tablespoon baking powder

½ teaspoon baking soda

¼ teaspoon salt

¼ cup butter

¾ cup low-fat buttermilk

2 tablespoons butter or vegetable oil spread, melted

Every time you fold and handle the dough, you develop the gluten, a protein made when flour and water combine. Overkneading makes biscuits tough.

Use a sharp-edged round cutter or glass to cut out the biscuits cleanly.

8. Remove from oven and let cool for a few minutes before serving.

Breakfast Strawberry Shortcakes

These are delicious at breakfast or *any* time of day.

Difficulty: Beginner / **Time:** 15 minutes + 1 hour to chill in refrigerator / **Makes:** 12

Steps

1. Using a serrated knife, carefully slice the biscuits in half and set aside.

2. Wash the strawberries and pat dry. Pull the leaves off the strawberries and discard.

3. Using a cutting board and a knife, cut the top off the strawberry and place cut side down on the cutting board. Slice the strawberries into ¼-inch slices and place in a medium bowl.

4. Sprinkle the strawberries with sugar and gently combine. Cover the strawberries and place them into the refrigerator for at least 1 hour.

5. To assemble, place one biscuit half on a plate. Spoon strawberries onto the biscuit and close with biscuit tops. Repeat.

6. Sift confectioner's sugar lightly over the tops of the biscuits. Garnish with a sprig of mint.

Ingredients

12 baking powder biscuits, cooled

18–24 strawberries

3 tablespoons sugar

1 tablespoon confectioner's sugar

12 sprigs mint (optional)

A good biscuit has a flaky structure, meaning that the butter (or fat) is spread in thin layers throughout the dough.

Picnic Time Carrot, Coconut, and Currant Bread

A very healthy gluten-free and milk-free snack for kids. Just eliminate the nuts for a child with tree nut allergies. This recipe is also vegan. Because a gluten-free batter is stickier, parchment paper is used to prevent sticking.

Difficulty: Intermediate / **Time:** 30 minutes to prepare +45–50 minutes to bake / **Makes:** 1 loaf, 12 slices

Ingredients

1½ **cups spelt flour**

2 **teaspoons baking powder**

½ **teaspoon baking soda**

½ **teaspoon salt**

2–3 **carrots**

1 **tablespoon flaxseed (you can substitute one egg if desired)**

½ **cup maple syrup**

¾ **cup almond milk**

⅓ **cup olive oil**

2 **teaspoons vanilla extract**

1 **teaspoon lemon juice**

1 **teaspoon cinnamon**

1 **teaspoon nutmeg**

½ **teaspoon ginger**

¼ **teaspoon cloves**

½ **cup finely chopped pecans**

½ **cup shredded coconut**

½ **cup currants**

Steps

1. Preheat the oven to 400°F (177°C). Line the bottom of a loaf pan with a piece of parchment paper. Using a pencil, trace the bottom of the pan on the paper and then cut out with scissors. Brush the loaf pan with vegetable oil and place the cutout parchment paper in the bottom of the pan.

2. Combine the flour, baking powder, baking soda and salt in a large bowl. Whisk together so the ingredients are well blended.

3. Wash and dry the carrots. Cut off the tops. Using a box grater, grate the carrots until you have 1½ cups.

4. In another bowl, add the carrots, flaxseed, maple syrup, almond milk, olive oil, vanilla extract, lemon juice, and spices. Mix until all ingredients are combined.

5. Add the carrot mixture to the flour mixture. Stir together with a wooden spoon until all the dry ingredients are absorbed by the liquid and there are no lumps. Fold in the chopped pecans, shredded coconut, and currants. Do not overmix the ingredients.

6. Pour the batter into your prepared pan. Place on the center rack in the oven.

Heat is more even in the middle of the oven so if you are baking just one item, put it there.

Dried currants look like small raisins and taste sweet and tangy.

7. Bake the bread for 45–50 minutes until a toothpick inserted into the middle of the loaf comes out clean and the bread is a golden brown. Allow the bread to sit in the pan to cool for 15 minutes.

8. Carefully run a knife along the sides of the pan to gently loosen the sides of the bread from the pan. Turn the bread out onto a wire rack and cool for another 15 minutes before slicing the bread. Serve as a perfect breakfast, picnic, or snack bread.

Protein-Packed Blueberry Pancakes

Nutritious and delicious, these pancakes will satisfy a breakfast or any-time-of-day appetite.

Difficulty: Intermediate / **Time:** 25 minutes / **Makes:** 10 3-inch pancakes

Ingredients

1 cup cooked quinoa
(⅓ cup raw)

¾ cup whole-wheat flour

¾ cup all-purpose flour

1 tablespoon sugar

2 teaspoons baking powder

1 teaspoon baking soda

⅛ teaspoon salt

2 eggs

1½ tablespoons lemon juice

1½ cups low-fat (2%) milk

1 teaspoon vanilla extract

3 tablespoons vegetable oil

1½ cups blueberries

Steps

1. Cook the quinoa according to the package instructions. Allow the quinoa to cool. Measure one cup of cooked quinoa and set it aside.

2. Mix both of the flours, sugar, baking powder, baking soda, and salt together in a large bowl.

3. Crack the eggs into a small bowl and beat lightly with a fork.

4. Pour the lemon juice into the milk and let it stand for 5 minutes.

5. In a medium bowl, add the eggs, soured milk, vanilla extract, and vegetable oil. Whisk the ingredients together until they are well blended.

6. Add the liquid ingredients to the flour mixture and stir. Be sure not to overmix the ingredients. There will be some lumps. Fold the quinoa and the blueberries gently into the batter.

7. Brush a griddle or frying pan with oil.

8. Place the griddle or frying pan on the burner and heat for about 2 minutes over medium heat.

9. Scoop batter into a ¼ cup dry measuring cup. Pour the batter onto the griddle and cook until bubbles appear and the pancake is golden brown underneath. Larger pans or griddles can hold up to four pancakes at a time.

10. Carefully turn the pancakes with a spatula. Cook the other side until golden brown, about 1 minute.

11. Serve the pancakes with your favorite topping.

Overmixing pancake batter makes tough pancakes. Stir just until the dry ingredients seem mixed in with the wet ingredients.

Video at http://www .wiley.com/go/ sciencechef.

Basic Muffins with Variations

Try this recipe as is, or be adventurous and try one of the eight variations.

Difficulty: Beginner / **Time:** 15 minutes to prepare +18–25 minutes to bake /
Makes: 12 muffins

Ingredients

cooking spray or 1 table-
spoon shortening

2 cups all-purpose flour

½ cup sugar

1 tablespoon baking powder

¼ teaspoon salt

2 eggs

1 cup low-fat (2%), reduced
fat (1%), or nonfat milk

¼ cup vegetable oil

Steps

1. Preheat oven to 375°F (190°C).

2. Lightly coat muffin cups with cooking spray or grease bottoms and sides of muffin cups with shortening.

3. Mix the flour, sugar, baking powder, and salt in a large bowl.

4. Mix the eggs, milk, and vegetable oil in a medium bowl.

5. Add milk mixture all at once to the large bowl with the flour mixture.

6. Combine ingredients with a wooden spoon just until all dry ingredients are moistened.

7. Fill each muffin cup two thirds full with batter. Do not overfill! If there is extra batter, make more muffins or mini-muffins (they will bake quicker).

8. Bake for 18–25 minutes at 375°F (190°C) or until golden brown and a toothpick inserted in the center comes out clean.

9. Remove from oven and place on wire rack. Let cool for 5 minutes.

10. Loosen muffins with rubber spatula and turn them out of the pan onto a rack to cool further.

Variations

Apple-Cinnamon Muffins: Add 1 teaspoon cinnamon and ¾ cup chopped apples to the dry ingredients in step 3.

Blueberry Muffins (pictured here): Add ¾ cup washed and dried blueberries to the dry ingredients in step 3. Gently mix together dry ingredients.

Cherry-Pecan Muffins: At the end of step 6, fold in ½ cup chopped dried cherries and ¼ cup chopped pecans.

Chocolate Chip Muffins: Add ¾ cup miniature chocolate chips in step 3.

Cornmeal Muffins: In step 3, reduce flour to 1 cup and add ¾ cup yellow cornmeal.

Oatmeal-Raisin Muffins: In step 3, reduce flour to 1½ cups and add ⅔ cup rolled oats. Add ½ cup raisins to the dry ingredients in step 3.

Peanut-Butter-and-Jelly Muffins: Spoon half the batter among 12 muffin cups. Place about 1 teaspoon peanut butter and ½ teaspoon jelly in each muffin cup. Cover each cup with remaining batter.

Whole-Wheat Muffins: In step 3, replace 1 cup of all-purpose flour with 1 cup white whole-wheat flour.

Don't overbeat muffin batter or the muffins will have large air pockets that look like tunnels inside them.

Use an ice cream scoop to fill the muffin tins.

Chapter 9

What Happens When You Beat Egg Whites or Cook Eggs?

~~~~~~~~~~~~~~~~~~~~~~~~~~~~~~~~

It is amazing to see how liquid egg whites can become light and fluffy and expand to many times their original size when they are beaten with a wire whip. Egg whites are mostly water but also contain **protein**, a nutrient found in every cell in your body. When you beat egg whites (cooks like to call this "whipping" rather than beating), you are actually beating air into them. The normally compact proteins found in egg whites unfold when whipped. As the proteins stretch out, they trap air bubbles. When proteins are made, they fold and twist themselves into a specific shape that allows them to do their jobs, but the act of whipping makes proteins unfold and untwist (a process called **denaturation**).

When whipping egg whites, pick an appropriately sized bowl because they increase over six times in size. Using an electric mixer or wire whip, start beating the egg whites at low speed until they look like foam. Then turn the speed up to medium or even medium-high. Do not beat on high speed. If the recipe says to beat until the whites form *soft peaks*, beat until the peaks form and flop over when the beaters are lifted up. As seen in the top photo, egg whites at soft peaks are still quite liquid and bubbly. For *stiff peaks*, continue to beat until the peaks stand up straight when the beaters are lifted. At this point, the egg whites almost look like whipped cream. Perform the next experiment to see for yourself.

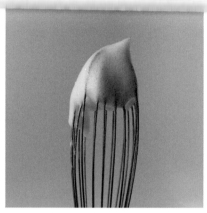

Soft Peaks

Stiff Peaks

Which Egg Whites Whip Up Faster?

Purpose: *To determine how egg temperature affects the whipping process.*

Materials

6 eggs, refrigerated

egg separator

2 mixing bowls

timer

electric mixer with wire whip

Procedure

1. Use an egg separator (as in photo) to separate three eggs. Put the egg yolks in the refrigerator (to use for cooking or baking) and leave the egg whites in a bowl at room temperature for 20 minutes. Set aside while you move on to step 2.

2. Using an egg separator, separate three more refrigerated eggs. Use an electric mixer with the wire whip attachment to beat these egg whites, but set a timer first so you know how long this step will take. Start at a low speed and after the whites get foamy, use medium-high speed to whip to stiff peaks. Note how much time it took to get stiff peaks.

3. Repeat step 2 with the egg whites at room temperature. Be sure to use the timer and note the time.

Observations

Record the answers to these questions in your *Science Chef Notebook* (see About This Book for how to set up your own notebook).

1. How long did it take the refrigerated egg whites to whip to stiff peaks?

2. How long did it take the room temperature egg whites to whip to stiff peaks?

3. Which egg whites whipped up faster?

All About Eggs

Beaten egg whites are used to give lightness and rising power to some cakes, pancakes, waffles, and soufflés (a light, fluffy baked egg dish). Some rules to follow whenever beating egg whites include these.

1. When separating the egg white from the yolk, be sure the yolk does not get in the whites. Yolks contain fat, and fat interferes with the ability of the proteins to foam and stretch around air bubbles.

2. Make sure the equipment you use to whip egg whites (such as the bowl and beaters) is perfectly clean. A glass or stainless steel mixing bowl is better than plastic because fat sometimes gets trapped in scratches inside plastic bowls.

3. A recipe may recommend that you add a small amount of cream of tartar or lemon juice to egg whites. Either will increase the volume of the egg whites when beaten.

4. If sugar is to be added, first beat the egg whites to the soft peak stage. Then add the sugar slowly while beating.

In addition, you can over-beat egg whites. For most recipes, stop whipping when the whites are smooth and glossy and just hold a peak when you lift the beater. If you overbeat egg whites, they go from being moist to very dry.

A whole egg contains the egg white and yolk. The yolk is high in water and protein. When whole eggs are heated up, their molecules speed up and collide with each other. The end result is that the proteins again unfold and lose their shape (or denature). The heat causes the liquid egg to first become semisolid and then continued heating removes more water and the eggs are firmer.

What Happened in the Experiment?

Egg whites foam up more easily and quicker when they are at room temperature. Specifically, when the proteins in egg whites are warmer, they are quicker to unfold and trap air.

The Best Veggie Quiche Recipe

Quiche is a pie crust filled with eggs, milk, cheese, and often vegetables or a protein such as ham.

Difficulty: Intermediate / **Time:** 25 minutes to prepare +45 minutes to bake / **Makes:** 8 servings

Steps

1. Preheat the oven to 375 °F (190 °C).

2. Soak the sun-dried tomatoes in a measuring cup filled with warm water for 10 minutes.

3. While they soak, wash the leek and cut in half lengthwise. Slice and chop the white part of the onion and place in a medium bowl.

4. Wash and chop the mushrooms, and place in the bowl.

5. Remove the tomatoes from the cup and pat dry. Slice and chop the tomatoes on a cutting board and place in the bowl.

6. Preheat a frying pan by placing it on a burner and setting to medium heat for 2 minutes. Add the oil and swirl to coat the bottom of the pan. Add the vegetables and sauté for 3 minutes and let cool.

7. Mix the vegetables with the cheese and place in the pie crust shell.

Ingredients

⅓ cup sun-dried tomatoes (not in oil)

1 medium leek

4 baby portabella mushrooms

1 tablespoon olive oil

1¼ cups shredded cheddar cheese

1 prepared pie shell, standard 9-inch size

¾ cup whole milk

6 eggs (or 1½ cups egg substitute)

¼ teaspoon salt

¼ teaspoon pepper

⅛ teaspoon nutmeg

When you cook eggs and milk together, a smooth semisolid gel called a custard is created.

As a custard bakes, the proteins in the eggs unfold and then come together to form a mesh that traps milk in a soft gel.

8. In another medium bowl, whisk together the milk, eggs, salt, pepper, and nutmeg.

9. Pour into pie shell over veggies and cheese.

10. Bake in the oven at 375 °F (190 °C) for 45 minutes until golden brown.

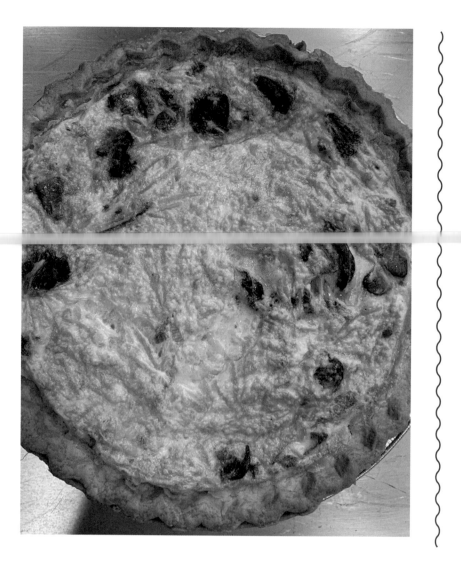

11. Allow quiche to cool for 10 minutes and cut into eight slices.

Custom Omelets

Omelets are a lot of fun because you can fill them with your own "custom" fillings. Try one!

Difficulty: Intermediate / **Time:** 20 minutes / **Makes:** 1 omelet

Ingredients

2 eggs

1 tablespoon milk (any type)

vegetable oil cooking spray

Steps

1. Crack eggs in a small bowl.

2. Beat eggs with a whisk and add milk.

3. Spray a medium frying pan.

4. Heat the frying pan over medium heat.

5. Pour the eggs into the frying pan. As the eggs set (firm) around the edges, use a heat-resistant rubber spatula to lift the edges and tilt the skillet to allow uncooked egg to flow underneath to get cooked.

6. When the eggs are almost set on the surface, fold in half and cook for 1–2 minutes longer. Slide omelet onto plate.

Variations

You can fill an omelet with almost anything you like. Just add the ingredient(s) before you fold the omelet in half. The photo shows a pizza omelet that was filled and is being folded.

Pizza: ¼ cup tomato sauce and 2 tablespoons shredded mozzarella cheese.

Western: ¼ cup chopped ham and 2 tablespoons sautéed chopped sweet bell pepper and onions.

Cheesesteak: 1–2 oz thinly sliced ribeye steak, 1 slice American cheese.

Country Garden: 2 tablespoons diced tomato, 1 tablespoon chopped broccoli, 2 tablespoons shredded cheese.

Stuffed Chicken: ¼ cup shredded chicken, 2 tablespoons shredded Swiss cheese, 3 small spinach leaves.

Use an 8-inch pan for a two-egg omelet so the cooking time is fast and you do not overcook the eggs.

Video at http://www.wiley.com/go/sciencechef.

Angel Food Cake

Angel food cake is a moist, airy cake with a sweet, delicate flavor. It is made in a tube pan—a deep baking pan with a hollow tube in the middle. The stiffly beaten egg whites allow the cake to rise without baking powder. This is one of the few cakes that have no fat.

Difficulty: Intermediate / **Time:** 30 minutes to prepare +1 hour to bake / **Makes:** 1 cake, 12 slices

Ingredients

12 eggs

1 cup cake flour

¾ cup confectioners' sugar

1 teaspoon cream of tartar

½ teaspoon salt

¾ cup confectioners' sugar

1 teaspoon vanilla extract

½ teaspoon almond extract

1 teaspoon lemon juice

Steps

1. Remove eggs from refrigerator 30 minutes before starting this recipe.

2. Preheat the oven to 325°F (165°C).

3. Stir the flour and ¾ cup sugar together in small bowl.

4. Crack eggs and, using an egg separator, separate whites from yolks. Place egg whites in a large, clean bowl.

5. Sprinkle the cream of tartar and salt over the egg whites.

6. Beat using a handheld or electric mixer until stiff peaks form. The egg whites should be shiny and moist.

7. Sprinkle some of the confectioners' sugar over the whites and gently fold in (over-and-under motion) with a rubber spatula. Repeat until all the sugar is mixed in.

8. Sprinkle the flour-sugar mixture on the egg whites and gently fold in. Repeat until all the flour and sugar is mixed in.

9. Fold in the vanilla and almond extracts and the lemon juice.

10. Gently fill an ungreased 10-inch tube pan with the batter.

11. Bake for 1 hour at 325°F (165°C). Test by pressing lightly in the center. The cake should spring back if it is done. If not, test at 5-minute intervals.

12. With oven mitts or pot holders, remove the cake from the oven and turn the pan over onto the neck of a glass (not plastic) bottle. Let the cake cool for 1½ hours.

13. When completely cooled, remove the cake from the pan by loosening the sides with a metal spatula.

> Cake flour feels softer than all-purpose flour because it contains less protein, which helps make cakes tender.

14. Serve with your favorite fruit.

Part 2

No More Boxes, Cans, or Jars:
Do It Yourself!

Chapter 10

Make-Your-Own Salad Dressings

~~~~~~

Salad dressings are liquids used to flavor and moisten salads. Many salad dressings are made of a vegetable oil and vinegar (or lemon juice) with additional ingredients to give it flavor. Vegetable oils commonly used in salad dressings include olive oil, soybean oil, or corn oil. Vinegar and lemon juice are acidic and make the salad dressing tangy. Vinegar and lemon juice are mostly water.

Oil and vinegar are substances that do not mix together. As seen in the top photo, the oil and vinegar stay separated when placed in a bowl. However, if you whisk oil and vinegar together, the oil will separate into small drops that stay evenly mixed through the dressing for a short time, as shown in the next photo. This type of mixture is known as a **suspension**. When the suspension of oil and vinegar stays still for a few minutes, the oil droplets once again cling together and separate from the vinegar.

Some easy-to-make salad dressings use dairy products, such as buttermilk, sour cream, or yogurt, instead of oil and vinegar. Other salad dressings use mayonnaise instead of oil and vinegar (such as ranch dressing). Mayonnaise-based dressings are thicker and creamier than those using oil and vinegar. Mayonnaise is made from egg yolks, vegetable oil, vinegar, lemon juice, and seasonings. Make your own mayonnaise in the following activity.

Make-Your-Own Mayonnaise

Purpose: *To make an emulsion that won't separate.*

Materials

medium bowl

2 egg yolks, large, room temperature

wire whip

½ teaspoon prepared mustard

¼ teaspoon kosher salt

1 cup vegetable oil (neutral color and flavor)

1 teaspoon white vinegar or lemon juice

Procedure

1. In a medium bowl, put the egg yolks. Using a wire whip, whisk the yolks until smooth and creamy, about 2 minutes.

2. Add the mustard and salt, and whip for 30 seconds or until the yolk is thick.

3. This is a crucial step. Whisking constantly, *slowly* drizzle in the oil a few drops at a time (see photo). Once the mayonnaise starts to thicken, that means the emulsion is starting to form. Now you can pour the oil in a thin stream while continuing to whisk vigorously.

4. Once the mayonnaise is at the right consistency, whip in the vinegar.

5. Cover bowl and place in refrigerator. Mayonnaise will keep for 1 week.

Observations

Record the answers to these questions in your *Science Chef Notebook* (see "About This Book" for how to set up your own notebook).

1. Observe the mayonnaise as you put it in the refrigerator. Is the oil separating from it?

2. Observe the mayonnaise 1 hour after you put it in the refrigerator. Is the oil separating from it?

Emulsions

Mayonnaise is an interesting substance because, even though it contains oil and vinegar, the oil never separates from the vinegar. This is because the egg yolk surrounds each drop of fat and prevents it from clumping or settling out of the mayonnaise. This is why mayonnaise is considered an **emulsion**. An emulsion is a stable mixture of two liquids that would normally separate from each other. A suspension does not have that stability, and the two liquids will separate from each other.

What Happened in the Activity?

The whisking action splits the oil droplets into smaller droplets, and the egg yolk surrounds the fat droplets so they don't clump together. There is no separation of oil at any time. Constant beating and the addition of oil in very small amounts help make and maintain the emulsion.

Trendy Tuna Salad

Tuna Salad can be eaten as a salad, on bread or crackers, or even in an ice cream cone. Add cooked macaroni to it and you'll have Macaroni and Tuna Salad—just top with fresh vegetables like cherry tomatoes.

Difficulty: Intermediate / **Time:** 15 minutes / **Makes:** 4 servings (1 scoop each)

Ingredients

2 cans (5 oz) tuna packed in water

1 small red onion (½ cup chopped)

1 celery rib (½ cup pieces)

3 tablespoons low-fat or homemade mayonnaise (see Make-Your-Own Mayonnaise)

2 tablespoons lemon juice

¼ teaspoon salt

¼ teaspoon white pepper

4 large lettuce leaves and 4 lemon wedges for garnish

Mayonnaise bought at the store is much more acidic than homemade mayonnaise so it lasts longer.

Steps

1. Open tuna cans and drain off the liquid. Put the tuna in a medium bowl.

2. Peel the outer papery skin off the red onion. Using a knife on a cutting board, cut the onion in half. Chop the onion into small pieces and add to the tuna.

3. Cut the ends off the celery rib. Cut the celery in half lengthwise. Cut across both pieces into ¼-inch pieces.

4. Add the celery, mayonnaise, lemon juice, salt, and pepper to the tuna and mix thoroughly.

5. Divide into four scoops. Serve each scoop on a lettuce leave and garnish with a piece of lemon.

Italian Dressing

Italian dressing is oil with vinegar, lime juice, or lemon juice that is seasoned. This recipe uses olive oil.

Difficulty: Beginner / **Time:** 15 minutes / **Makes:** 15 1-tablespoon servings

Steps

1. Combine the olive oil, lime juice, vinegar, oregano, salt, white pepper, garlic powder, onion powder, and sugar in a small bowl.

2. Remove the outer skin from the onion. Using a knife on a cutting board, slice the onion in half and wrap up half of the onion in plastic wrap and put in the refrigerator. Slice the remaining onion half, then chop the onion into small pieces. Measure 1 teaspoon of onion and add to the small bowl.

3. Cover the bowl with plastic wrap and refrigerate. This dressing will keep for up to 7 days.

Ingredients

½ cup olive oil

4 tablespoons lime juice

2 tablespoons white wine vinegar

¼ teaspoon oregano

¼ teaspoon salt

¼ teaspoon white pepper

½ teaspoon garlic powder

½ teaspoon onion powder

¼ teaspoon sugar

1 teaspoon chopped onion

Always add dressings to greens just before serving or eating. Oils in the dressings are soaked up by the leaf, creating soggy greens.

Video at http://www.wiley .com/go/ sciencechef.

Rich Raspberry Dressing

This dressing gets its name and distinctive flavor from raspberry vinegar. Vinegar is one of the world's oldest cooking ingredients. Vinegars may be flavored with herbs or fruit flavorings such as rosemary, chile pepper, lemon, or raspberry.

Difficulty: Beginner / **Time:** 10 minutes / **Makes:** 10 1-tablespoon servings

Ingredients

2 tablespoons olive oil

½ cup raspberry vinegar

1 teaspoon sugar

¼ teaspoon salt

Steps

1. Combine the olive oil, vinegar, sugar, and salt in a small bowl and mix well.

2. Cover the bowl with plastic wrap and refrigerate. This dressing will keep for up to 5 days.

Layered Lunchtime Salads in a Jar

This is a great recipe for making a salad ahead of time and it is easy to pack for work or school.

Difficulty: Intermediate / **Time:** 25–30 minutes / **Makes:** 2 salads

Steps

1. Wash canning jars thoroughly in warm, soapy water and dry.

2. Peel the carrot. Using a knife and a cutting board, cut the carrot into ¼-inch coins and cut in half again.

3. Cut the pepper into strips and then into ½-inch pieces.

4. Cut the tomato into wedges.

5. Slice the cucumber into ¼-inch slices and cut in half. Set all vegetables aside.

6. Open canned corn and drain the liquid and measure.

7. Wash greens and set aside.

8. To assemble the salad, add ¼ cup of your favorite salad dressing to each canning jar.

Ingredients

Large carrot

½ red or green pepper

1 small tomato

½ cucumber

½ cup corn

1 cup salad greens (such as spring mix)

½ cup of Italian or Rich Raspberry dressing in this chapter (or use your favorite)

2 16-oz canning jars with lids

9. Layer each jar with the carrots, pepper, tomato, cucumbers, and corn and top with salad greens.

10. Secure the lids on the jars. The Lunchtime Salad in a Jar can last in the refrigerator up to 5 days.

Variations

Additional ideas for Layered Lunchtime Salads.

Layer 1: your favorite dressing

Layer 2: tomatoes, cucumbers, red onion, asparagus, celery, peppers, carrots

Layer 3: mushrooms, zucchini, beans, lentils, peas, corn, broccoli

Layer 4: boiled eggs or cheese (feta, gouda, cheddar, etc.)

Layer 5: rice, pasta, quinoa, or couscous

Layer 6: nuts and greens such as lettuce, spinach, or arugula

Default Delicious Three Bean Salad

Three Bean Salad is a collection of three different kinds of beans in an oil-and-vinegar dressing. The beans are usually green beans, wax beans, and kidney beans, but you could use any cooked bean or partially cooked vegetable instead.

Difficulty: Intermediate / **Time:** 20–25 minutes plus 2 hours to refrigerate / **Makes:** 8 servings

Steps

1. Open the cans of kidney beans, green beans, and wax beans. Empty the cans into a colander to drain the liquid.

2. Remove the outer skin of the onion. Using a knife on a cutting board, cut the onion in half and chop.

3. Cut the ends off the celery rib. Cut the celery rib in half lengthwise and then cut the celery into ¼-inch pieces.

4. Combine the vinegar, oil, salt, and pepper in a small bowl.

5. Put the three kinds of beans and the chopped onion into a medium bowl. Pour the oil and vinegar dressing over the beans.

6. Cover with plastic wrap and refrigerate for 2 hours before serving. This salad will keep for up to 7 days.

Ingredients

15- or 16-oz can kidney beans

14.5-oz can green beans

14.5-oz can wax beans

1 medium onion
(1 cup chopped)

1 rib of celery (½ cup pieces)

⅓ cup cider vinegar

2 tablespoons vegetable oil

¼ teaspoon salt

⅛ teaspoon pepper

Kidney beans are large beans that are usually red, but some are white. They are a favorite in salads and also in Mexican and Italian cooking.

Cider vinegar is made from fermented apple juice and smells of apples.

Paninis with Mayo Pesto Dressing

A panini is an Italian grilled sandwich. It can be cooked in a frying pan, like a grilled cheese sandwich, or using a panini grill. A panini grill (sometimes called a panini press) has top and bottom plates that press and grill the sandwich in one step. Both top and bottom plates have ridges in them that give this sandwich its distinctive appearance.

Difficulty: Intermediate / **Time:** 30 minutes plus 10 minutes to grill / **Makes:** 2 sandwiches

Ingredients

3 tablespoons low-fat or homemade mayonnaise

1 tablespoon pesto sauce (recipe in Chapter 11)

1 medium zucchini

½ medium red onion (½ cup sliced)

Vegetable oil spray

5–6 tablespoons olive oil, divided

⅛ teaspoon salt

⅛ teaspoon pepper

1 roasted red pepper

4 slices ciabatta (1 oz each)

4 slices of cheddar, American, or provo-lone cheese

Steps

1. Preheat oven to 400°F (205°C).

2. Whisk the mayonnaise and pesto sauce together in a small bowl to make the mayonnaise and pesto dressing.

3. Wash the zucchini. On a cutting board with a knife, slice a zucchini lengthwise into four to six pieces.

4. Peel off the papery skin of the red onion and cut the onion in half. Slice into ½-inch rings. Wrap the other half of the onion in foil or plastic wrap and refrigerate.

5. Place the vegetables on a cookie sheet lined with foil and lightly sprayed with vegetable oil spray. Brush vegetables lightly with 2 tablespoons of the olive oil. Sprinkle with salt and pepper.

11. Place sandwiches in panini maker or frying pan and cook sandwich for about 5 minutes on each side. Remove and cut sandwich in half and serve. Garnish with multigrain chips and a pickle.

6. Place the tray in the oven for 10 minutes or until the vegetables are tender when you test with a fork. Take out of the oven with oven mitts and let cool.

7. Meanwhile, cut the roasted red pepper in half and trim the edges so it fits onto the sandwiches.

8. Spread pesto mayo on two slices of bread.

9. Build the sandwiches with cheese, zucchini, onion, and roasted red peppers.

Pesto is an Italian sauce with ingredients such as olive oil and basil leaves, which give it its distinctive green color.

Ciabatta bread is an Italian white bread with a firm, crisp crust and a soft interior with holes.

10. Cover each sandwich with a second piece of bread and brush the panini grill or frying pan with the 1–2 tablespoons of olive oil. Preheat the grill according to the manufacturer's directions. Brush the top of each sandwich with 1 tablespoon of olive oil.

Fresh Fruit Cocktail with Honey Yogurt Dressing

This is a delicious and fun way to eat fresh fruit!

Difficulty: Intermediate / **Time:** 20 minutes / **Makes:** 4 servings

Ingredients

1 cup plain low-fat yogurt

2 tablespoons honey

1 tablespoon lemon juice

¼ teaspoon ground ginger

1½ tablespoons grated orange peel

½ pint raw strawberries (1 cup sliced)

1 cup blueberries

1 14-oz can pineapple chunks

1 cup precut honeydew melon

1 cup precut cantaloupe

4 small bowls or glass tumbler

Small skewers

> When the flesh of a fruit is exposed to air, oxygen in the air reacts with enzymes in the fruit to make it turn brown. Vitamin C in the lemon juice prevents the browning.

Steps

1. Combine the yogurt, honey, lemon juice, and ginger in a small bowl and mix well.

2. Grate the orange peel and mix it with the rest of the ingredients.

3. Wash the strawberries and blueberries. Pat dry with a paper towel.

4. On a cutting board with a knife, slice the tops off of the strawberries. Slice each strawberry into 3–4 pieces. Combine the strawberries, blueberries, pineapple, and melons together in a large bowl.

5. Place ¼ cup of honey yogurt dressing at the bottom of four tumblers. Top with fresh fruit mixture. Place a skewer in each cup.

Chapter 11

Grow-Your-Own Herbs

~~~~~~~~~~~~~~~~~~~~~~~~~~~~~~

Many of the foods we eat, such as pasta sauces, are flavored and seasoned with herbs and spices to make them taste good. **Herbs**, such as oregano used on pizza, come from the leaves of plants. Spices come from other parts of the plant such as the bark, root, or fruit. **Spices** are almost always dried, whereas many herbs can be bought fresh at the supermarket or grown at home.

The main parts of a plant include the roots, stem, and leaves. The **roots** absorb water and nutrients from the soil and keep the plant firmly anchored to the ground. The **stem** supports the plant and carries water and nutrients to the leaves. In a process called **photosynthesis**, the **leaves** use sunlight, carbon dioxide in the air, and water to make their own food and also oxygen. Many, but not all plants, have flowers as well.

Many flowers develop **fruits**, such as apples, that contain seeds for new plants. Get your fingers in the dirt and grow your own herbs in the following activity.

Plant an Indoor Herb Garden

Purpose: *To grow a plant from seed.*

Procedure

1. Plant seeds ¼-inch deep and 4 inches apart in potting soil in flowerpot. (Feel free to choose different herbs than the ones listed.)

2. Water thoroughly and place in a location that is NOT too bright. Keep the soil moist but not saturated with water. Check the pots daily for growth. In about 2 weeks, the plant will break through the soil (thyme may require a few more days).

3. Once the plants emerge, put them in a location that gets at least 6 hours of sun daily. A south-facing window gets the most hours of sun throughout the year. If you are growing chives, an east- or west-facing window is better as chives thrive with less intense light and cooler temperature.

4. Water consistently. Certain herbs prefer very well-drained soil (including thyme and oregano) so let the soil dry out a little between waterings. Other herbs like more moisture, and it's best to keep the soil slightly moist but not soggy.

5. Feed occasionally. To promote healthy growth, use a plant fertilizer following the product's directions.

6. By 6–8 weeks, you can pinch off leaves and use them in cooking—they will grow back quickly. Frequent harvesting with herb snips encourages fresh growth, as does pinching 2–3 inches off the stem tips. Remove any flower buds before they open to prolong leaf growth.

7. Use the fresh basil leaves, for example, in recipes to provide a pleasant, spicy flavor. Fresh basil

Materials

2 basil seeds (bush basil stays small)

2 mint seeds (peppermint is a favorite)

2 thyme seeds (English, French, or lemon thyme have sturdier stems, making it easier to remove the tiny leaves)

3 flowerpots (6 inches wide), saucers to go underneath the pots

potting soil

leaves can also be wrapped in aluminum foil and frozen for up to 6 months. Fresh mint leaves can be chopped up and used in brownies, salad dressings, and other foods. Fresh mint can also flavor tea and other beverages but is generally removed after brewing the tea. Fresh thyme leaves are used in many meat and vegetable dishes.

Observations

Record your answers to the following questions in your *Science Chef Notebook* (see "About This Book" for how to set up your own notebook).

1. Write down your observations of the plants at the end of: Week 1, Week 2, Week 3, Week 4, Week 5, and Week 6.

2. At Week 8, has your plant produced any flowers?

Common Herbs and Spices

Here are a few common herbs and spices.

- Basil is known as the "tomato herb" because it gives tomatoes an excellent flavor. It is used to season other vegetables such as zucchini, squash, carrots, and cabbage. Basil also can be added to soups, stews, and many other dishes.

- Oregano, another herb, was almost unknown in the United States until after World War II, when the servicemen stationed in Italy brought back a taste for Italian dishes containing oregano. Today oregano, with its pungent, spicy flavor, is one of the most popular herbs in this country (see photo). Oregano is used to flavor tomato sauce, spaghetti sauce, pizzas, and other Italian dishes.

Oregano plant

- Cinnamon is a spice that comes from the bark of cinnamon or cassia trees. Cinnamon sticks are the dried-out bark that has curled up. Cinnamon is used in baking and desserts.

Cloves and nutmeg are native to Indonesia. Cloves are the dried unopened flower buds of a tropical tree, and nutmeg is the seed of the fruit of the nutmeg tree. Both are used in baking and desserts.

Whole cloves

Cinnamon sticks

What Happened in the Activity?

It will take about 6–8 weeks for the basil plant to grow big enough for you to pinch off leaves for cooking. Once the seed is in the soil and gets plenty of water, it gets to work on sending roots into the soil and the top of the plant will sprout from the soil with tiny leaves (called **germination**). Once these leaves begin to make food, the plant becomes a **seedling**, or young plant, and will further develop its roots and leaves. When the roots can support growth, the **vegetative stage** begins and you will see growth over the weeks in the stem, branches, and leaves. The final stage of growth is the **reproductive stage** when the plant starts to produce flowers that contain tiny seeds.

Oregano   Chives   Mint

Garden Fresh Tomato Sauce

Difficulty: Intermediate / **Time:** 30–40 minutes / **Makes:** 8 half-cup servings

Make this old favorite without opening a can! It's not hard!

Ingredients

6–8 fresh plum tomatoes (£1)

1 medium onion
(1 cup chopped)

vegetable oil cooking spray

½ teaspoon sugar

½ teaspoon dried
basil leaves

¼ teaspoon garlic powder

2 fresh basil leaves
(optional garnish)

Steps

1. Heat at least 5 inches of water in saucepan until it boils. Plunge tomatoes into boiling water for 30 seconds. Be careful not to let the water splash you.

2. Remove the tomatoes with a large spoon and put them in a colander. Rinse in cold water. Remove the skins with your hands or a paring knife on a cutting board. Chop the tomatoes into small pieces.

3. Remove the outer skin of the onion. Using a knife on a cutting board, cut the onion in half and chop.

4. Spray a large frying pan with cooking spray. Heat the frying pan over medium heat for 1 minute.

5. Sauté the onion in the frying pan for 3–4 minutes. Add tomatoes, sugar, basil, and garlic powder to the frying pan.

6. Simmer for 15–20 minutes to cook and blend flavors. Be careful not to overcook.

Variation

Meat Sauce: Brown ½ pound lean ground beef, chicken, or turkey in step 5 with onion. Drain any fat before going on to the next step.

7. Roll up fresh basil leaves like a cigar. Take a kitchen shears and snip basil into ¼-inch slices for the garnish.

8. Serve sauce over cooked pasta (such as gluten free) and garnish with freshly cut basil.

When tomatoes cook, some of the water they contain turns to steam. With less water, the sauce will thicken.

Video at http://www.wiley .com/go/ sciencechef.

Creamy Blender Pesto Sauce

While making this easy sauce, cook your favorite pasta.

Difficulty: Beginner / **Time:** 20–25 minutes / **Makes:** 6 half-cup servings

Ingredients

2 cups firmly packed basil leaves

¼ cup grated parmesan cheese

¼ cup pine nuts

1 clove garlic

2 tablespoons almond milk

2 teaspoons lemon juice

½ cup olive oil

⅛ teaspoon salt

⅛ teaspoon pepper

Steps

1. Wash basil leaves and pat dry.

2. In a blender combine basil, cheese, pine nuts, garlic, almond milk, lemon juice, olive oil, salt, and pepper.

3. Blend at medium speed until mixture is smooth.

4. Pour sauce over hot pasta and mix thoroughly. Serve with extra parmesan cheese.

Pine nuts are small seeds from one of several pine tree varieties. They have a sweet, faint pine flavor.

Pesto can be made 1 day ahead, covered tightly, and refrigerated.

Roasted Red Pepper Pesto Sauce with Artichokes, Olives, and Tomatoes

Use a food processor to make this sauce quickly!

Difficulty: Intermediate / **Time:** 20–30 minutes / **Makes:** 4 servings

Steps

1. Cook your favorite pasta using the package directions.

2. In a food processor, combine the peppers, pine nuts, nutritional yeast, lemon juice, garlic, salt, and pepper. Process the ingredients until smooth.

3. On a cutting board with a paring knife, cut the cherry tomatoes in half.

4. Mix cooked hot pasta and red pepper pesto sauce in a large mixing bowl.

5. Add the tomatoes, black olives, and artichoke hearts to the pasta and gently mix.

Ingredients

4 cups cooked pasta

3 large roasted red peppers, jarred variety (8 oz)

¼ cup pine nuts

2 tablespoons nutritional yeast (or parmesan cheese)

2 tablespoons lemon juice

2 large garlic cloves

¼ teaspoon salt

¼ teaspoon pepper

¾ cup cherry tomatoes

¾ cup pitted black olives

1 cup canned artichoke hearts

You can substitute lightly cooked broccoli for the artichoke hearts.

Nutritional yeast is inactive yeast and is popular in vegetarian cooking to add a cheesy flavor to dishes.

Chapter 12

Make-Your-Own Fermented Foods

~~~~~~

One way to make pickles is by using a process called fermentation. **Fermentation** is when small organisms, such as bacteria or yeast, convert complex molecules into simpler ones. Bacteria are tiny organisms that you can't see but are everywhere. Most do not harm us. Fermentation has been used for thousands of years to make bread from flour, wine from fruit juice, beer from grains, yogurt and sour cream from milk, and sauerkraut from cabbage. Kimchi, a traditional Korean side dish, is made from fermented vegetables.

When yeast is used to make bread, the yeast feeds on sugars and starches in the bread dough. After eating the sugars and starches, the yeast make carbon dioxide gas that makes bread rise. Otherwise, bread would be pretty flat. Bacteria used in making yogurt feed on the sugars in the milk to produce acids that give yogurt a tart taste and makes it thick.

Wine uses both yeast and bacteria while beer just uses yeast. In beer, yeast eats the sugars in the grains to produce alcohol. Chocolate is made from cacao beans that must be fermented, dried, and roasted to get the flavor of chocolate.

Some fermented foods still have live bacteria—such as yogurt, sauerkraut, and sour dill pickles. The bacteria used in fermentation have many benefits: they seem to make foods easier to digest, boost the immune system, and help us maintain a healthy weight.

Use Bacteria to Make Yogurt from Milk

Purpose: *To use bacteria from yogurt to make a fermented food.*

Materials

Heavy pot or Dutch oven with lid

2 quarts whole milk

Instant-read thermometer or candy thermometer

3 tablespoons *plain* **whole milk yogurt (make sure the container states it contains live and active cultures)**

Procedure

1. Put cold water in the bottom of the pot or Dutch oven and swish it around. Dump out the water.

2. Add the milk to the pot or Dutch oven. Using a medium to medium-high heat, bring the milk to a low simmer with bubbles forming around the edge.

3. Heat the milk to right below boiling: 180 °F (82 °C) to 195 °F (90 °C). Use a thermometer clipped onto the pot (such as a candy thermometer) or test the temperature frequently with an instant-read thermometer. *Stir the milk occasionally and gently as it heats to make sure the milk doesn't stick to the bottom of the pan and burn.* This step kills any unwelcome bacteria and also helps thicken the milk.

4. Once the temperature is reached, remove the pot from the heat. Fill the sink with ice and cold water and put the pot on the ice to cool down. Cool the milk to lukewarm—precisely 110 °F (43 °C) to 115 °F (46 °C)—checking frequently with a thermometer.

While it is cooling, stir occasionally to prevent a skin from forming on top and to cool the milk evenly.

5. Once the temperature is reached, take 1 cup of milk from the pot and place in a small bowl. Whisk in the yogurt until smooth. Stir the yogurt-milk mixture back into the pot to spread the good bacteria throughout the milk.

6. The next step, called incubation, requires the milk to stay at a consistent, lukewarm temperature for 4–9 hours. To keep the milk lukewarm, cover the pot with a lid, wrap the pot in a large towel, and move to a warm place, such as the oven with the oven light turned on. You could also set up a cooler filled with warm water (right around 110 °F or 43 °C) and put the pot in there.

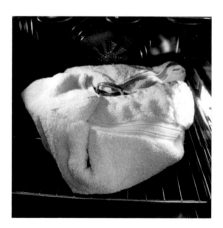

7. During this time, avoid stirring the yogurt until it is completely set. The bacteria from the store-bought yogurt will eat the sugar in the milk and produce acids. The acids help thicken the milk and give it a tart flavor. The longer it sits, the thicker and more tart it becomes. Check the flavor and consistency of the yogurt at 4 hours.

8. Once the yogurt has a flavor and consistency you like (often at 8 hours), you can stir it and transfer to storage containers. Cover and refrigerate. The refrigerator will thicken it up a little more. The yogurt will stay fresh for 10 days.

Observations

Record your answers to the following questions in your *Science Chef Notebook* (see "About This Book" for how to set up your own notebook).

1. Describe the flavor and consistency of the yogurt at 4 hours.

2. How many hours of incubation were needed to produce a yogurt with the flavor and consistency you wanted?

Making Pickles

Fermented pickles rely on salt and beneficial bacteria on the skin of the cucumber to make things happen. The first recipe in this chapter uses a short fermentation period to produce bread-and-butter pickles. Traditional dill pickles are made by fermenting cucumbers in salty water. But not all pickles are made by fermentation. In the second pickle recipe, pickles are made by pouring a hot vinegar mixture over the cucumbers. To make either recipe, you will need glass canning jars with lids.

What Happened in the Activity?

The good bacteria from the yogurt convert the sugar in milk to lactic acid, which thickens the milk and gives it a tangy taste. Lactic acid denatures some of the protein in milk, meaning that the proteins lose their special shapes and curdle, so the milk becomes thicker. The first time you make homemade yogurt it will likely taste quite tart, no matter how long it was incubated. This is because you are used to store-bought yogurts that are sweetened. In time, your taste buds will adapt to homemade yogurt. But if you'd like to sweeten the yogurt, you can add fresh fruit, dried fruit, or honey.

Aunt Teresa's Old-Fashioned Bread-and-Butter Pickles

These pickles start to ferment when covered with salt overnight. Friendly bacteria, known as lactic acid bacteria, naturally live on vegetables such as cucumbers. But don't scrub the cucumbers too hard as that removes some of the bacteria needed to start the fermentation process.

Difficulty: Intermediate / **Time:** 35 minutes to prepare +1 day to refrigerate +45 minutes to put in jars / **Makes:** 10 jars

Steps

1. Wash and dry the cucumbers. Slice cucumbers and onions. Place in a large pot (not aluminum) or large bowl and cover with salt. Mix the salt throughout the pickles and onions with your hands. Cover and place in refrigerator overnight.

2. Preheat the oven to 200 °F (95 °C). Place the jars and lids on a tray and place in the oven for 10 minutes to sterilize. Do not put seals in the oven. Remove the tray and let it sit to cool.

3. Wash the cucumbers in batches to remove the salt. Change the water three or four times and taste to make sure the cucumbers are not too salty before proceeding. If they are, wash them again.

Ingredients

10 16-oz canning glass jars with lids

6 quarts Kirby cucumbers or about 24–25 Kirby cucumbers (4 cucumbers make one quart)

6 medium onions, sliced

¾ cup kosher salt

6 cups white vinegar

6 cups sugar

⅓ cup mustard seed

1 tablespoon celery seed

1½ teaspoons turmeric

until small bubbles form. Do not bring to a boil. This takes about 10–15 minutes.

7. Spoon mixture into pickle jars. Use a funnel to get cucumber pieces into the jar and then spoon liquid over the cucumbers.

4. If you haven't sterilized the jars and lids in the oven, you can place them in a large canning pot. Fill pot with water and bring to a boil to sterilize the jars. Boil for 10 minutes. Carefully remove with tongs and set aside on a towel.

5. In a large pot, mix the remaining ingredients (from vinegar to turmeric) and bring to a boil. Boil for 5 minutes.

6. Add the cucumbers to the mixture and continue to simmer

8. Fill the liquid to the top of the jars. Place lids on top. Lids will "pop" when all of the air is out of the jar and pickles are done.

9. When cooled slightly, tighten the lids to seal. They do not require a water bath as the vinegar and sugar mixture serves as a preservative to protect the cucumbers.

Kirby cucumbers are best for pickling because they are small and not covered with wax that would interfere with pickling.

Compared to the small, fine crystals in table salt, kosher salt has large, rough crystals.

Cool Crunchy Refrigerator Pickles

These pickles are quicker to make. Instead of using fermentation, refrigerator pickles rely on vinegar for that traditional pickle taste.

Difficulty: Intermediate / **Time:** 45 minutes to prepare +1 day to refrigerate / **Makes:** 4–6 jars

Steps

1. Preheat the oven to 200 °F (95 °C). Place the jars and lids on a tray and place in the oven for 10 minutes to sterilize. Do not put seals in the oven. Remove the tray and let it sit to cool.

2. Wash and dry the cucumbers. With a cutting board and knife, cut the ends off each cucumber. Cut in half lengthwise and cut each half into three or four slices, forming spears. Set aside.

3. In a large pot, combine the white vinegar, water and pickling spices. Bring the mixture to a low boil and stir for about 10 minutes. Turn off the heat and let the mixture cool.

4. Pack the cucumber spears tightly into the canning jars.

Ingredients

- wide mouth 16-oz canning jars and lids
- 6 medium Kirby pickling cucumbers
- 1 cup white vinegar
- 2 cups water
- ¼ cup pickling spices
- 1 garlic bulb
- 1 small bunch fresh dill

5. Peel the papery skin off the garlic cloves. Place one garlic clove and one sprig of dill in each jar.

6. Pour the cooled liquid over the cucumbers and place the seals and lids on the jars. Tighten the lids.

7. Refrigerate pickles for 24 hours before opening the jar. Store in the refrigerator. Refrigerator pickles will keep for about a month.

Pickling spice is a mix of spices, such as cloves and dill seeds, that are great for pickling.

Video at http://www.wiley.com/go/sciencechef.

Chapter 13

Make-Your-Own Smoothies

Smoothies are mixtures. **Mixtures** are a combination of substances that do not react chemically with each other, such as sand in water or the ingredients in a soft drink. Mixtures can be solids, liquids, or gases. There are two types of mixtures: homogeneous or heterogeneous.

- In a **homogeneous mixture,** the ingredients are all evenly distributed throughout the mixture—such as salt in water. Salt in water is a special type of homogeneous mixture called a **solution** because the salt *dissolves* in the water. A solution contains a solute and a solvent. The solute is the dissolved substance, such as salt. The solvent is the substance that does the dissolving. Water acts frequently as a solvent.

- In a **heterogeneous mixture,** the substances are not well mixed or evenly distributed—such as chocolate chips in cookie batter. There are lots of chocolate chips in certain parts of the batter but few in other parts. Sand in water is also a heterogeneous solution—when you mix it up, the mixture looks homogeneous but the sand will settle to the bottom when left alone.

To summarize, a homogeneous mixture is very well mixed and looks uniform. Heterogeneous mixtures are not as well mixed.

Viscosity is the resistance of a fluid, such as a mixture, to flow. A fluid with low viscosity, such as water, flows easily because its molecular makeup results in little friction as it flows. Molasses has a greater viscosity than water and flows much more slowly. Test the viscosity of fluids in the following experiment.

Test the Viscosity of Fluids

Purpose: *To compare the viscosity of different substances.*

Materials

Clear cups

2 marbles

Apple juice and honey

Corn oil (or other vegetable oil) and soda

Water and applesauce

Procedure

1. Put equal amounts of apple juice and honey into clear cups. Make sure you have about 2 inches of fluid in each cup.

2. Hold a marble in each hand and release on top of the cups at the same time. Note which marble hits the bottom first.

3. Perform steps 1 and 2 using corn oil and soda.

4. Perform steps 1 and 2 using water and applesauce.

Observations

Record your answers to the following questions in your *Science Chef Notebook* (see "About This Book" for how to set up your own notebook).

1. Which marble reached the bottom first—in the apple juice or honey?

2. Which marble reached the bottom first—in the corn oil or soda?

3. Which marble reached the bottom first—in the water or applesauce?

4. Which three substances were the most viscous?

Smoothies and Heterogeneous Mixtures

Smoothies are a type of heterogeneous mixture called a **suspension**. To understand what a suspension is, first let's look at the ingredients for a banana almond smoothie.

- 1 cup almond milk
- 1 frozen peeled banana, broken into 3–4 chunks
- ¼ cup almond butter
- ⅛ teaspoon almond extract

After the smoothie is mixed up in a blender, it looks well mixed and the banana and almond butter are dispersed throughout the liquid. However, the banana and almond butter do not dissolve and are suspended just temporarily in the almond milk. Once this smoothie sits for a short time, the banana and almond butter will separate from the almond milk and start to settle at the bottom due to their weight—a key characteristic of a suspension.

The above shows a smoothie that has started to separate. You can see that the top of the drink is lighter in color than the bottom of the glass where some of the ingredients are settling. You can recognize a suspension if you can see particles such as orange juice pulp in orange juice or gas bubbles in a soft drink. Keep in mind that homogeneous mixtures look the same throughout.

What Happened in the Experiment?

The marble fell the fastest in water or the fluids containing the most water: apple juice and soda. The marble took longer to get through the honey, corn oil, and applesauce, which are thicker and more viscous (resistant to flowing).

Vita-Packed Tri-Berry Smoothie

Difficulty: Beginner / **Time:** 15 minutes to prepare / **Makes:** 2 servings

Ingredients

½ cup yogurt, nonfat, plain

½ cup water or ice cubes (if using ice cubes, add last)

1 banana

5 strawberries

¼ cup blueberries

¼ cup raspberries

1 tablespoon honey

1 cup spinach

The order in which you add ingredients to the blender makes a difference. Add the liquid ingredients first, then fresh fruits, frozen fruits, leafy greens, and ice.

The ice goes in last to help push the other ingredients down into the blades for even mixing.

Steps

1. Wash and dry all fruits and spinach.

2. On a cutting board with a knife, cut each strawberry in half.

3. Place all ingredients in the blender in the order listed above.

4. Blend all ingredients until smooth for about 1 minute. If you would like a thinner consistency, add 2–3 tablespoons of water or milk and blend again.

"Tropicalicious" Island Mango Smoothie

Difficulty: Beginner / **Time:** 15 minutes to prepare / **Makes:** 2 servings

Steps

1. Place all ingredients in the blender in the order listed above.

2. Blend ingredients until smooth for about 1 minute. If you would like a thinner consistency, add 2 to 3 tablespoons of orange juice and blend again.

Ingredients

½ cup yogurt, nonfat, plain

½ cup orange juice

1 medium banana

¼ cup raspberries

1 peeled orange

½ cup fresh frozen mango pieces

½ cup fresh frozen pineapple chunks

1 tablespoon honey

1 tablespoon sweetened coconut

Using frozen fruit creates a rich and sweet tasting smoothie without the need for ice or added sugar.

Video at http://www.wiley.com/go/sciencechef.

Green-n-Lean Warrior Smoothie

Difficulty: Beginner / **Time:** 15 minutes to prepare / **Makes:** 2 servings

Ingredients

¾ cup almond milk

¼ cup water

1 medium banana

½ cup fresh frozen mango pieces

1 cup fresh frozen pineapple chunks

5 strawberries (½ cup)

1 tablespoon honey

1 teaspoon chia seeds

1 cup packed spinach leaves

Use baby spinach rather than regular spinach for less spinach flavor.

Bananas help neutralize bitter flavors.

Steps

1. Wash and dry the strawberries and spinach leaves. On a cutting board with a knife, cut each strawberry in half.

2. Place all ingredients in a blender in the order listed above.

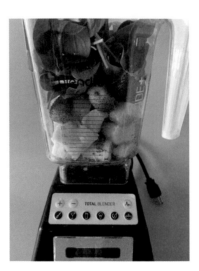

3. Blend ingredients until smooth for about 1 minute. If you would like a thinner consistency, add 2 to 3 tablespoons of water or almond milk and blend again.

Chapter 14

Make-Your-Own Popsicles

~~~~~~

Everyone knows that ice pops are made of ice, but have you ever thought about what ice really is? Ice is a **solid**, one of three common **phases of matter**. Ice has weight and holds its shape. A substance is in the solid phase when it is at low temperatures. When ice melts, it changes to water, a liquid. **Liquids** are another phase that appears between the solid and gas phases. Liquids also have weight and take up space, but they don't have a shape of their own. Instead a liquid will take the shape of its container. When water boils, it changes to steam, a gas. **Gas** still has weight and takes up space, but it has no shape. Gas will take both the shape and volume of the container it is in. A substance is in the gas phase when it is at a high temperature.

As temperatures go up, water molecules move faster, and indeed at 212 °F (100 °C) water turns to steam, which has a lot of energy. As temperatures go below 32 °F (0 °C), water's molecules move more slowly and actually hook onto each other to form solid crystals. Do the following activity to learn more about ice and ice crystals.

Test What Happens When Water Turns to Ice

Purpose: *To observe the physical changes when water turns to ice.*

Procedure

1. Pour the water into the paper cup.

2. Using a pen or pencil, mark how high the water is on the inside of the cup.

3. Put the cup of water in the freezer for 2 hours, then observe.

Observations

Record your answers to the following questions in your *Science Chef Notebook* (see "About This Book" for how to set up your own notebook).

1. Open the freezer and take out the cup. Where is the top of the ice in relation to the line you drew?

2. What happens when water freezes to ice?

Ice

Ice, the solid phase of water, has some unique properties. When you put water in the freezer, ice

Materials

¼ cup water

small paper cup

pen or pencil

crystals form and the water expands and gets bigger. Ice is less dense than water, so ice cubes float at the top of your drinks. The fact that ice floats on water is important for fish and other organisms that live in lakes and ponds during the winter. Ice actually insulates the water so the water stays just above a freezing temperature.

This chapter contains three recipes for popsicles. To make popsicle, you can use a popsicle mold or simply use 3-oz paper or plastic cups. You will need wooden popsicles sticks when using paper or plastic cups or if your popsicle mold doesn't come with sticks.

What Happened in the Activity?

As ice crystals start to form in the water, the water expands by about one eleventh. This expansion causes the top of the ice cube to be higher than the line drawn. The same process occurs when food is packed into freezer containers so it is always important to allow extra space for expansion.

Fruity Popsicles

This recipe is for basic fruit juice and fresh fruit on a stick. Pick your favorites!

Difficulty: Beginner / **Time:** 15–20 minutes to prepare, 6–7 hours to freeze /
Makes: 6 3-oz popsicles

Steps

1. Add 2 teaspoons of fruit into each of 6 paper/
   plastic cups or molds (use 3-oz cups or molds).

2. Pour the juice evenly into each cup or mold. Do
   not fill to the top—leave about ¼ inch of space.

3. Put the cups/molds in the freezer for 45 minutes.
   Then remove from the freezer and insert a
   wooden or plastic stick into the center of the cup/
   mold. Do not insert the sticks all the way in.

4. Freeze about 6 hours or until hard. To loosen the
   pop in a paper cup, hold onto the stick and peel off
   the paper cup. Hold a plastic cup or mold under
   warm running water for a few seconds before
   pulling out the pop. Silicone molds release easily.

Ingredients

¼ cup fresh or canned fruit
packed in its own juice such
as diced peaches

2 cups of your favorite juice,
such as apple juice

You can
also use ice
cube trays or
muffin tins lined
with foil cupcake
wrappers in place of a
popsicle mold.

Video at http://
www.wiley.com/
go/sciencechef.

Yogurt-Fruit Swirl Popsicles

These popsicles blend fruit and yogurt. You can use any type of yogurt and any type of fruit to make your own delicious combination.

Difficulty: Beginner / **Time:** 15–20 minutes to prepare, 6 hours to freeze / **Makes:** 4 3-oz popsicles

Ingredients

¾ cup fresh blueberries or ¾ cup sliced strawberries or 1 medium banana

1 teaspoon honey (optional)

1 cup low-fat/nonfat vanilla yogurt

Steps

1. If using fresh fruit, wash in a colander. For strawberries, use a paring knife to remove the leafy green top of each strawberry and the pale flesh right underneath it. Then slice each strawberry. Remove the skin of the banana and cut into five pieces.

2. Place the fruit in a blender or food processor and turn on low to purée the fruit. To **purée** means to crush a food so it turns into a thick liquid.

3. Put the fruit purée in a bowl. Blend in 1 teaspoon honey if the puréed fruit is a little tart. Gently swirl in 1 cup vanilla yogurt to keep the pretty swirls.

4. Pour into four paper/plastic cups or popsicle molds (3 oz each). Insert a wooden or plastic stick into the center of the cup/mold. Do not insert the sticks all the way in.

5. Freeze about 6 hours or until hard. To loosen the pop in a paper cup, hold onto the stick and peel off the paper cup. Hold a plastic cup or mold under warm running water briefly (a few seconds) before pulling out the pop. Silicone molds release easily.

Variations

After filling each mold half full, add 1 to 2 teaspoons of granola or chocolate chips. Then fill each mold to the top and freeze as directed.

Always use ripe fruit to get a sweet popsicle. Use any fresh fruit in season.

Pudding Popsicles

You can make pudding using an instant mix and then pour it into cups or molds for a frozen treat on a hot summer day. For a vanilla-and-chocolate pop, make both vanilla and chocolate puddings and pour equal amounts into each cup. For a marbled effect, move the blade of a table knife around the cup.

Difficulty: Beginner / **Time:** 15–20 minutes to prepare, 5 hours to freeze / **Makes:** 6 5-oz popsicles

Ingredients

vegetable oil cooking spray

2 cups low-fat (1%) or nonfat milk

1 package instant pudding mix, vanilla, chocolate, or butterscotch (3.4 oz)

You can also use ready-made pudding.

Because the pudding mix is pretty thick, it may be easier to use a pastry bag or a freezer bag with a corner snipped off to fill the molds.

Steps

1. Lightly spray the inside of plastic/paper cups or molds with vegetable oil cooking spray.

2. Beat milk and pudding mix with a wire whip for 2 minutes.

3. Spoon into molds, leaving some room at the top. Insert a wooden or plastic stick into the center of the cup/mold. Do not insert the sticks all the way in.

4. Freeze about 5 hours or until hard. To loosen the pop in a paper cup, hold onto the stick and peel off the paper cup. Hold a plastic cup or mold under warm running water briefly before pulling out the pop. Silicone molds release easily.

Variations

Fill the cup or mold half full. Add 1–2 teaspoons whipped cream and/or crushed Oreo cookies, nuts, or peanut butter cups. Then fill each mold to the top, and freeze as directed.

Chapter 15

Make-Your-Own Power Cookie Mix

There are many different forms of sugar at the supermarket: white sugar, brown sugar, powdered or confectioners' sugar, corn syrup, molasses, and honey. Sugar also occurs naturally in foods such as fruits, honey, vegetables, and milk. The sweetness found in ripe fruits, for example, comes from the simple sugar **fructose**. Honey is made by bees and includes the simple sugars fructose and **glucose**. Glucose is very important in the body as it is always running around in your blood providing a source of energy to the body's cells. Vegetables and milk may not taste sweet, but they do contain some **natural sugars**.

Foods that contain natural sugars.

Examples of added sugars:

White sugar

Brown sugar

Powdered sugar

Unlike natural sugars that occur naturally in some foods, **added sugars** are sweeteners that are added to foods and beverages (such as soft drinks, cookies, and candy) for sweetening and flavor. A well-known added sugar is table sugar (white sugar), which is over 99% sucrose, a double sugar. Table sugar is made from the juice of the sugarcane plant or the sugar beet. If you look closely at table sugar, you will notice that is made of sugar **crystals** shaped like cubes. Sugar crystals are orderly arrangements of sucrose molecules. Make sugar crystals and learn more about solutions in the following activity.

Make Sugar Crystals

Purpose: *To see how sugar crystals precipitate from a solution.*

Materials

1 cup water

small saucepan

2 cups sugar

12-inch piece of string

straw or pencil

paper clip

glass jar

magnifying lens (optional)

Procedure

1. Put one cup of water in the saucepan. Place on high heat and bring to a boil. Turn heat to medium.

2. Add sugar, about ¼ cup at a time, and stir until no more sugar will dissolve. The water should dissolve between 1½ and 2 cups of sugar.

3. Remove the saucepan from the burner and turn the heat off. Let cool for 10 minutes.

4. Tie one end of the string to a straw or pencil. Tie the paper clip to the other end of the string so that the clip just dangles above the bottom of the jar when the straw is placed over the top of the jar. Put the string into place.

5. Pour the sugar water into the jar. Put the jar in a place where it won't be disturbed for 1–2 days.

6. Within 24–48 hours, look in the jar to see if crystals have formed on the string or elsewhere.

Observations

Record your answers to the following questions in your *Science Chef Notebook* (see "About This Book" for how to set up your own notebook).

1. Did crystals form on the string within 1–2 days?

2. Describe what you see in the jar and on the string.

Sugars and Health

Sugars that occur naturally in foods are excellent ways to take in sugar because it is packaged with other important nutrients such as vitamins, minerals, and often **fiber**, a health-promoting **carbohydrate**. The more added sugars you consume, the more likely you are to be overweight and have other health issues such as heart disease and diabetes. Sweets, such as cookies, are okay to eat but need to be eaten in moderation.

What Happened in the Activity?

When you first added sugar to the boiling water, the sugar crystals dissolved, making a **solution**, a homogeneous mixture of two or more substances. When as much sugar had been dissolved as possible, the solution was saturated. A **saturated solution** contains the maximum concentration of a solute (in this case, sugar) dissolved in the solvent (in this case, water). But the saturation point changes depending on the *water temperature*. *Hot water can dissolve and hold more sugar than cold water*. So as the solution cooled, sugar came out of the solution and formed crystals on the string. The crystals are known as a **precipitate**, a solid that forms out of a solution.

Power Cookie Mix

This cookie mix is easy to make and used to make the cookie recipes that follow. Once you have a batch of this mix in the refrigerator, it's a snap to bake up your favorite cookies whenever you like.

Difficulty: Intermediate / **Time:** 15 minutes to prepare / **Makes:** 14 cups (about 5 batches of cookies)

Steps

1. Using a table knife on a cutting board, cut the butter into small pieces. Put butter in a large bowl.

2. Add 4½ cups flour to the bowl with the butter.

3. Using a food processor, add half of the flour and butter mixture to the bowl and process until the butter looks like small peas. Remove from bowl. Repeat with the remaining flour and butter. If you would prefer to use two table knives, hold a knife in each hand, draw the knives across each other to cut through the butter and dry ingredients. If using a pastry blender, cut through the butter and dry ingredients and keep cutting until the flour and fat mixture is in pieces about the size of small peas.

4. Add 4½ cups flour, powdered milk, baking powder, sugar, and salt to the flour and fat mixture. Stir together.

5. Pour the mix into a container with a tight lid and put into the refrigerator. The mix can be stored in the refrigerator for up to 5 weeks.

Ingredients

2 cups butter

4½ cups all-purpose flour

4½ cups all-purpose flour (used twice)

2 cups powdered milk

⅓ cup baking powder

¼ cup sugar

1 tablespoon salt

It is *very important to be super accurate in your measurements in baking.* Using a little too much or too little of an ingredient can greatly affect whether your baked good comes out right.

Video at http://www.wiley.com/go/sciencechef.

Peanut Butter Cookie Treats

Peanut butter cookies are a mouthwatering classic!

Difficulty: Beginner / **Time:** 15 minutes to prepare + 12 minutes to bake / **Makes:** 2 dozen cookies

Ingredients

vegetable oil cooking spray

⅓ cup peanut butter

⅔ cup sugar

1 egg

1 teaspoon vanilla extract

1 tablespoon water

1½ cups Power Cookie Mix

3 tablespoons sugar

If you're baking multiple pans of cookies at once, rotate the pans midway through the bake: top to bottom, bottom to top; front of the pan to the back, back to the front.

Always preheat the oven and keep the door closed as much as possible!

Steps

1. Preheat the oven to 375 °F (190 °C). Spray the cookie sheets with vegetable oil cooking spray.

2. Mix the peanut butter and sugar together in a medium bowl.

3. Add the egg, vanilla extract, and water to the peanut butter mixture. Stir well.

4. Add the Power Cookie Mix to the peanut butter mixture and stir well.

5. Roll the dough into 1-inch balls. Roll the balls in sugar on a flat surface. Then flatten the balls with the bottom of a drinking glass.

6. Place the pieces of cookie dough on a cookie sheet and make an *X* with the tines of a fork on the top of each piece of dough. The traditional mark on peanut butter cookies is the hash sign.

7. Bake at 375 °F (190 °C) for about 10 to 12 minutes or until golden brown.

8. Using oven mitts, remove the cookie sheet from the oven and let the cookies cool for about 5 minutes. Remove the cookies with a spatula.

M&M Cookies

This is a versatile cookie dough that can be used with M&M chocolate candies, chocolate chips, or other chips, as well as raisins and apples.

Difficulty: Beginner / **Time:** 15 minutes to prepare +14 minutes to bake / **Makes:** 3 dozen cookies

Steps

1. Preheat the oven to 375 °F (190 °C). Spray cookie sheets with vegetable oil cooking spray.

2. Place the Power Cookie Mix in a medium bowl. Set aside.

3. Mix dark brown sugar, egg, water, and vanilla extract together in a small bowl. Add the sugar-egg mixture to the Power Cookie Mix and stir just until well blended.

4. Fold M&Ms into Power Cookie Mix.

5. Drop the cookie batter by teaspoonfuls onto cookie sheet.

6. Bake at 375 °F (190 °C) for about 12 to 14 minutes or until golden brown. After 5 minutes, switch cookie pan positions in oven for even baking.

7. Using oven mitts, remove the cookie sheet from the oven and let the cookies cool for about 5 minutes. Remove the cookies with a spatula.

Ingredients

vegetable oil cooking spray

3 cups Power Cookie Mix

¾ cup dark brown sugar

1 egg

⅓ cup water

½ teaspoon vanilla extract

1½ cups M&M® brand chocolate candies

Instead of M&Ms, you can substitute:

1½ cups of chocolate chips

1½ cups peanut butter chips

1 cup diced apple and ½ cup raisins

Major Molasses Cookie Bites

This recipe uses mostly molasses for sweetening. Molasses is a dark, thick syrup created when sugar is made from sugar cane or sugar beets.

Difficulty: Beginner / **Time:** 15 minutes to prepare + 14 minutes to bake / **Makes:** 4 dozen cookies

Ingredients

vegetable oil cooking spray

4 cups Power Cookie Mix

¼ cup sugar

½ cup brown sugar

1 teaspoon cinnamon

1 teaspoon ginger

½ teaspoon cloves

1 egg

1 cup molasses

To keep baked goods fresh, wrap tightly in plastic to prevent air from pulling moisture from the baked good (which makes it dry).

Steps

1. Preheat the oven to 375°F (190°C). Spray the cookie sheets with vegetable oil cooking spray.

2. Put the Power Cookie Mix, sugar, brown sugar, cinnamon, ginger, and cloves in a medium bowl. Mix until combined.

3. Whisk together the egg and molasses in a small bowl until well blended.

4. Put the egg mixture into the bowl with the mix. Stir just until well blended. Drop cookie batter by teaspoonfuls onto cookie sheet.

5. Bake at 375°F (190°C) for about 12–14 minutes or until golden brown.

6. Using oven mitts, remove the cookie sheet from the oven and let the cookies cool for about 5 minutes. Remove the cookies with a spatula.

Delicious Double Chocolate Honey Brownies

This recipe uses honey as the sweetener.

Difficulty: Beginner / **Time:** 15 minutes to prepare +20–25 minutes to bake / **Makes:** 16 brownies

Steps

1. Preheat the oven to 350 °F (180 °C). Spray a 9-inch × 9-inch baking pan with vegetable oil cooking spray.

2. Put the Power Cookie Mix, honey, and cocoa in a medium bowl. Mix well.

3. Place butter or vegetable oil stick in the microwave dish and cover. Microwave for 30–60 seconds, until melted and bubbly. Let cool for 1 minute before removing cover.

4. Add the melted fat, egg, water, and vanilla extract to the bowl with the mix. Mix thoroughly.

5. Fold chocolate chips or M&Ms into the batter. Pour the batter into the pan.

6. Bake at 350 °F (180 °C) about 20 minutes or until lightly browned. Cool before cutting into squares.

Ingredients

vegetable oil cooking spray

1 cup Power Cookie Mix

⅔ cup honey

½ cup unsweetened cocoa

¼ cup butter or vegetable oil stick

1 egg

¼ cup water

1 teaspoon vanilla extract

1 cup mini chocolate chips

or

1 cup M&M® brand chocolate candies

Light colored, shiny baking pans produce the best results as they conduct heat evenly. Dark pans absorb heat and don't bake as evenly.

Chapter 16

Make-Your-Own Nut Butter

~~~~~~

Most nuts are seeds of long-lived trees such as pistachio trees. The drawing shows a branch of a pistachio tree with nuts that are ripening. Nuts are unique in that they have hard shells and store their energy as fat, not glucose. Nuts are nutritious and a good source of healthy fats and also protein. Examples of nuts include almonds, cashews, hazelnuts, macadamia nuts, pecans, pine nuts, pistachios, and walnuts. The largest nut is actually the nut that grows inside a coconut on a palm tree.

Despite its name, peanuts are not actually nuts. They do contain a lot of fat and they are a seed, but they don't grow on trees. Instead the peanut plant grows above ground and the peanuts grow just under the ground attached to the plant.

Nuts need little or no cooking before being eaten. Most nuts you buy at the store have been cooked, usually roasted in oil. Roasted nuts are crunchier, tastier, and darker in color. You can also buy raw nuts.

When nuts are ground, the nut's oil transforms the nuts from a crunchy snack to a creamy nut butter. **Oils** are fats that are liquid at room temperature, such as almond oil or peanut oil. Almonds and peanuts are both about 50% oil so their nut butters are essentially tiny pieces of nuts floating in oil.

Compare the Freezing Point of Oils Such as Peanut Oil

Purpose: *To demonstrate the concept of freezing point (the temperature at which a liquid turns into a solid).*

Materials

¼ cup soybean oil (usually labeled "vegetable oil")

¼ cup peanut oil

2 small clear plastic cups

Marker

Procedure

1. Pour ¼ cup of soybean oil into one cup and label the cup.

2. Pour ¼ cup peanut oil into the other cup and label it.

3. Place in the coldest part of the refrigerator.

Soybean Oil   Peanut Oil

4. In 2 hours, remove the cups from the refrigerator. Which one appears to be more solid?

Observations

Record your answers to the following questions in your *Science Chef Notebook* (see "About This Book" for how to set up your own notebook).

1. Describe the appearance of the soybean oil and the peanut oil.

2. Which oil appears more solid?

Freezing Points of Oils

When you make peanut butter at home, for example, or buy a "natural" peanut butter at the store, every time you open the jar, there is a layer of peanut oil on the top. When a jar of natural peanut butter sits in a cabinet, the peanut oil naturally separates to the top of the jar, leaving the solids at the bottom. Then you have to stir the oil back into the solids every time you want to use it. One solution to this problem is to store the jar upside down, which forces the peanut oil to trickle through the peanut solids.

Another solution to this problem is to stir the oil into the peanut solids and then refrigerate the peanut butter. Peanut oil has a freezing point of 37 °F (3 °C), which is about the temperature in your refrigerator. Freezing point is the temperature at which a liquid turns into a solid. As the temperature decreases, it becomes more solid. Warm peanut oil is a liquid, but in a cold refrigerator it will become more solid, and this will stop the separation of the oil from the solids.

What Happened in the Experiment?

The peanut oil in the refrigerator is more solid than the soybean oil. Soybean oil has a freezing point of 3 °F (−16 °C) so it won't even start to turn solid until the temperature is much lower than the refrigerator. Peanut oil has a freezing point of 37 °F (3 °C), which is found in most refrigerators, so the peanut oil started to change over to a solid from a liquid.

Homemade Honey-Roasted Peanut Butter

Making your own peanut butter is fast and easy. You can substitute maple syrup for the honey in this recipe if you prefer.

Difficulty: Intermediate / **Time:** 20 minutes to prepare / **Makes:** 16-oz jar, about 16–1.5 tablespoon servings

Ingredients

1 24-oz bag unsalted roasted peanuts in shells (or 3 cups dry-roasted unsalted peanuts)

2 teaspoons sea salt

2 teaspoons honey

2 tablespoons peanut oil

Steps

1. Shell the peanuts into a medium bowl. Remove the skin and measure out three cups of peanuts.

2. Place peanuts, sea salt, and honey into the bowl of a food processor.

3. Pulse the food processor until the peanut mixture resembles sand and the peanuts are ground. The mixture will not be creamy yet.

4. Process the peanuts again and slowly pour the peanut oil into the peanut mixture. Continue processing the peanut butter until smooth.

5. Store peanut butter in an air-tight container or a mason jar in the refrigerator. Peanut butter will keep for about 2 months.

Video at
http://www
.wiley.com/go/
sciencechef.

The Best Banana Almond Milkshake

Just blend up these favorite foods—bananas, almond milk, and ice cream—with ice and some flavorings and you have a delicious and nutritious snack.

Difficulty: Beginner / **Time:** 10 minutes to prepare / **Makes:** 2 1-cup servings

Ingredients

½ medium banana

½ teaspoon vanilla extract

1 cup ice cubes

1 cup almond milk

½ cup vanilla ice cream

⅛ teaspoon cinnamon or nutmeg

Steps

1. Place all ingredients in a blender except the cinnamon and blend until smooth.

2. Pour the milkshake into a tall glass and sprinkle with cinnamon or nutmeg and serve.

"Peanutty" Coco-Chocolate Energy Treats

These treats are great for grab-and-go healthy snacks.

Difficulty: Beginner / **Time:** 30 minutes to prepare / **Makes:** 18 energy treats
(1 serving = 2 treats)

Steps

1. Place the oats in a blender and process on a high speed until a fine oat flour is formed.

2. In a large bowl, mix together the peanut butter, oil, honey, vanilla extract, and salt with a wooden spoon. Slowly add the oat flour into the peanut butter mixture and continue to mix the ingredients together.

3. When the mixture is just about mixed, fold the chocolate chips and 2 tablespoons shredded coconut into the dough.

4. Roll dough into approximately 1-inch balls. At this time, balls can be rolled in 1 cup shredded coconut if desired.

Ingredients

2 cups rolled oats

2 tablespoons peanut butter

2 tablespoons vegetable oil

¼ cup honey

1 teaspoon vanilla extract

½ teaspoon sea salt

2 tablespoons mini dark chocolate or white chocolate chips

2 tablespoons finely shredded coconut

1 cup finely shredded coconut (optional)

> **Rolled oats are partially cooked—they have been steamed and rolled to flatten them.**

5. Place the energy treats on a cookie sheet lined with foil or parchment paper and freeze for about 10 minutes. Then, place treats in a zipper-lock bag and store in the freezer or refrigerator.

Easy Cashew Fettuccini with Sun-Dried Tomatoes and Chives

This recipe features another nut butter—cashew butter. It blends very well with the other ingredients to make a tasty sauce over fettuccini noodles. If you use a gluten-free pasta, this dish will be gluten free.

Difficulty: Intermediate / **Time:** 2 hours soaking time + 35–40 minutes to prepare / **Makes:** 4 servings

Steps

1. Place the cashews in a large measuring cup or a bowl. Cover the cashews with warm water and let them soak for 2 hours. Drain the cashews.

2. While the cashews soak, place the sun-dried tomatoes in a small bowl and cover with warm water. Allow tomatoes to soak for 20 minutes and drain.

3. Place the cashews, arrowroot powder, nutritional yeast, garlic cloves, sea salt, pepper, and half of the almond milk in a food processor and process until smooth.

4. On a cutting board, slice the sun-dried tomatoes into long, thin strips. If using fresh chives, wash the chives and snip into ¼-inch pieces using kitchen scissors. Set aside.

5. In a large saucepan filled with water, bring water to a boil. Add ½ teaspoon of salt and cook the pasta according to the directions on the package, about 10 minutes or until tender.

6. Place a colander in the sink and drain the pasta.

Ingredients

1¼ cup cashews

6 sun-dried tomatoes, not in oil

1 tablespoon arrowroot powder (or 2 teaspoons cornstarch)

4 tablespoons nutritional yeast (or 2 tablespoons parmesan cheese)

3 garlic cloves

1 teaspoon sea salt

½ teaspoon white or black pepper

2½ cups almond milk or 2% milk

2 teaspoons dried chives (or 1 small bunch fresh chives)

½ teaspoon salt

10 oz of fettuccini noodles

3 tablespoons grated parmesan cheese

7. In a large sauté pan, pour the cashew mixture into the pan. Add the remaining almond milk.

8. Add the pasta, sun-dried tomatoes, chives, and the parmesan cheese to the sauté pan and toss to cover with the sauce. (If using fresh chives, save some to use as a garnish.)

9. Transfer the pasta to a large bowl, garnish with remaining fresh chives, and serve.

Chapter 17

Make-Your-Own Jam

~~~~~~

At the supermarket, there's always a section of jelly, jam, and preserves. These products are made from fruits and each one is different in some way.

- *Jelly* is a clear fruit spread made from fruit juice and sugar.

- *Jam* is thicker than jelly because it contains real fruit. It is made from equal weights of sugar and chopped, crushed, or puréed fruit that is cooked until very soft.

- *Preserves* are another fruit spread made from sugar and large chunks of the fruit or the whole fruit (like berries). Preserves are chunkier in texture than jelly or jam and often contain the seeds found in fruits such as strawberries.

The photo compares jelly, jam, and preserves. As you can see, the jam is thicker than the jelly, and the preserves, actually strawberry preserves, contain strawberry seeds.

Jelly   Jam   Preserves

When making jelly, jam, or preserves, the recipe may call for pectin, which is used for its ability to thicken. **Pectin** is a substance found in the cell walls of almost all plants. The **cell wall** is found around each plant cell where it works to protect and support the cell. There are tiny holes in the cell wall so that water and nutrients are shared between cells. Pectin helps support the plant and keep it strong. Pectin also plays a role in fighting microorganisms, such as certain bacteria, that can harm the plant.

Fruits contain varying amounts of natural pectin, and overripe fruits contain less pectin than ripe fruits. Citrus fruits, like oranges and lemons, are very high in pectin. Grapes or cranberries are rich enough in pectin to make their own jelly, jam, or preserves. Other fruits, such as peaches or strawberries, are low in pectin. You can buy powdered (or liquid) pectin, which is made by extracting it from fruits. Learn more about pectin in the following experiment.

Pectin

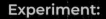

Compare Pectin Content of Fruits

Purpose: *To test fruits to see which contains more pectin.*

Procedure

1. Cut 1 cup of grapes into quarters and place in small saucepan. Add 2 tablespoons water.

2. Heat grapes and water to boiling, then reduce heat. Continue to simmer for 15 minutes. Turn off heat.

3. Measure 1 teaspoon of grape juice from the saucepan and place in a paper cup. Let cool for several minutes.

4. Measure 1 teaspoon of orange juice with pulp into another cup.

5. Measure 1 teaspoon of apple juice into the last cup.

Grape juiceorange juice with pulpapple juice

6. Add 1 tablespoon of rubbing alcohol to each cup. Carefully swish the liquids around the cup for 1 minute. **Do NOT taste this mixture.** Let stand for 2 minutes.

Materials

1 cup grapes

paring knife

cutting board

small saucepan

wooden spoon

3 small paper cups

1 teaspoon orange juice with pulp

1 teaspoon apple juice

3 tablespoons of rubbing alcohol

7. Observe how much (if any) jelly-like material formed in each cup.

WARNING: Rubbing alcohol is NOT edible. Once you are done, throw out the cups and their contents immediately.

Observations

Record your answers to the following questions in your *Science Chef Notebook* (see "About This Book" for how to set up your own notebook).

1. How much jelly-like material formed in the cup with the grape juice, orange juice, and apple juice?

2. Which cup had the most jelly-like material?

Pectin and Colloids

When small particles (such as pectin) are added and dispersed in a liquid, a **colloid** is formed. Colloids are heterogeneous mixtures (see Chapter 13)

in which the dispersed particles are *bigger* than those found in solutions. When pectin is added to a liquid mixture of fruit, its long pectin molecules thicken the fruit mixture by bonding to each other. This bonding makes a kind of net that traps the liquid from the fruit and prevents the liquid from moving easily. Fruit jelly or jam is actually a special type of colloid, called a **gel**. Gels are mostly liquid but behave like solids. At high temperatures, a gel is liquid, but at colder temperatures, a gel is solid. Indeed, when you let freshly made jam cool down, it will become more solid.

Sugar, of course, gives sweetness to jelly, jam, and preserves. But sugar helps in other ways, too. Sugar works with pectin to help thicken the jam. Sugar also helps prevent spoilage because it forms chemical bonds with the water, so the water is not available to support the growth of harmful microorganisms. In addition, sugar helps the product maintain its flavor and color.

What Happened in the Experiment?

If pectin is present, the rubbing alcohol causes a chemical reaction that creates a semisolid gel in the cup. This means that enough pectin is present to form a pectin gel. Grapes are high in pectin and a gel does form in that cup. Some gel also forms in the orange juice with pulp, but no gel forms in the apple juice. When apples are processed to make clear juice, the juice is free of pectin and other cell wall components. Because both the grape juice and orange juice contained some fruit pulp (meaning some plant cells), and both fruits are good sources of pectin, a pectin gel formed in both cups.

Jammin' Red Raspberry Jam

It's important to measure the mashed berries and sugar carefully
so the jam will be the right consistency.

Difficulty: Intermediate / **Time:** 60 minutes / **Makes:** 64 2-tablespoon servings

Steps

1. Wash jelly jars and lids in hot soapy water, and rinse thoroughly with warm water. Place on a towel to air dry.

2. With a potato masher, crush one cup of whole raspberries at a time. Remeasure the raspberries after they are crushed, and add four cups of crushed raspberries to a large Dutch oven.

3. Stir in the sugar until it completely dissolves. Add the lemon juice and stir again.

4. Bring the mixture to a boil over medium high heat and boil for 1 minute. Lower the heat.

5. Stir in the butter and liquid pectin and boil again on medium-high heat for one more minute. Turn off the heat.

Ingredients

8 eight-ounce jelly jars with lids (or 16 four-ounce jelly jars with lids)

6 quarts raspberries

6½ cups sugar

1 tablespoon lemon juice

1 teaspoon butter

⅔ cup liquid pectin

6. Using a wooden spoon, skim off any foam that is on the top of the jam mixture.

7. Ladle the jam into the jars filling up to ¼-inch below the rim. Wipe the jar rim using a clean, damp cloth to remove any jam on the rim. Carefully place on lids and screw bands.

8. When the mixture slightly cools, tighten the screw bands. Shortly you will hear the tops making a popping sound, which means all the air is out of the jar and the jam is almost set. Let the jam sit undisturbed for 24 hours until cooled and store in your pantry or refrigerator.

Sugar absorbs moisture, which makes it hard for microorganisms to survive in jam or jelly.

Video at http://www .wiley.com/go/ sciencechef.

Whole-Wheat Snickerdoodle Surprise Muffins

This recipe is half whole-wheat flour and half white flour to give you the benefits of whole grain and good taste. The surprise in these muffins is some raspberry jam in the middle.

Difficulty: Intermediate / **Time:** 20 minutes to prepare + 25 minutes to cook

+25 minutes to ~~~~~~~~~~~~~~~~~~~~~~~~~ **Makes:** 12 muffins

Steps

1. Preheat the oven to 350 °F (175 °C).

2. Spray a muffin tin with vegetable oil cooking spray.

3. In a large bowl, mix together the flours, sugar, baking powder, spices. and salt.

4. In a separate bowl, whisk the egg, almond milk, olive oil, and vanilla extract together.

5. Make a well in the middle of the dry ingredients. Pour the almond milk mixture into the well and stir the wet and dry ingredients together until well blended. Do not overmix.

6. Fill each muffin cup ⅔ full of batter. Put 1 teaspoon of jam in the center of the muffin and cover it with an additional heaping tablespoon of batter. The batter should come to within about ¼ inch of the top of each muffin cup.

7. Bake the muffins at 350 °F (175 °C) for 18–20 minutes or until an inserted toothpick comes out clean.

8. Cool muffins for 10 minutes on the top of the stove. Take the muffins out of the tin and cool for an additional 15 minutes on a cooling rack.

9. In the meantime, melt the vegetable oil spread in the microwave. In a small separate bowl, mix the cinnamon and decorative sugar together.

Ingredients

vegetable oil cooking spray

1 cup all-purpose flour

1 cup whole wheat flour

⅔ cup light brown sugar

2 teaspoons baking powder

½ teaspoon cinnamon

¼ teaspoon nutmeg

½ teaspoon salt

1 large egg

1 cup almond milk

⅓ cup olive oil

1 teaspoon vanilla extract

¼ cup of your favorite jam

For the Topping (optional):

2 tablespoons vegetable oil spread

½ teaspoon cinnamon

¼ cup large crystal sugar

10. To finish the muffins, use a pastry brush and lightly brush the top of the muffin with the melted vegetable oil spread. Sprinkle generously with cinnamon sugar.

The best balsamic vinegar is made from the juice of white grapes and aged in wooden barrels for 12 years.

Chicken Breasts Glazed with Peach Jam

You can use any type of jam in this recipe.

Difficulty: Intermediate / **Time:** 20 minutes to prepare +30 minutes to cook / **Makes:** 4 servings

Steps

1. Preheat the oven to 350°F (175°C).

2. Lay plastic wrap on the counter. Place the chicken on it and then place additional sheets of plastic wrap on top of the chicken. Gently pound the chicken breasts so that they are all about the same height and will therefore cook evenly.

3. Place the chicken in a 13-inch × 9-inch baking pan. If using butter, melt it in a bowl with a cover in the microwave. Brush chicken with the melted butter or olive oil. Sprinkle with salt and pepper. Bake for 15 minutes.

4. Combine the peach jam with the mustard and vinegar and stir together thoroughly.

5. Remove the chicken after 15 minutes and use a brush to glaze the chicken breasts. Bake for 15 minutes longer or until the chicken reaches 165°F (75°C) when you use an instant-read thermometer. Serve.

Ingredients

4 boneless chicken breast halves, skinless

1 tablespoon olive oil or butter

½ teaspoon salt

¼ teaspoon pepper

¾ cup peach jam

1 tablespoon spicy mustard

1 teaspoon balsamic vinegar

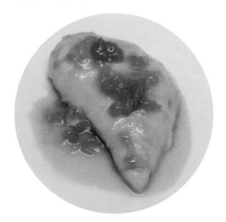

Chapter 18

Make-Your-Own Dried Fruits

~~~~~~

All foods, even dry crackers, contain some water. Raw fruits and vegetables are high in water. In fact, watermelon is about 93% water (by weight), and many lettuces are at least 90% water! Much of the water is found inside the plant's cells. Drying foods (called **dehydration**) is a process in which some of the water in a food is removed.

Water is very important for plants for several reasons.

1. In order for a seed to grow into a plant, it needs a lot of water.

2. Plants also need water to make **glucose**, a sugar that provides a source of energy for the plant. Glucose is made during the process of **photosynthesis** that also requires sunlight and carbon dioxide (in the air).

3. Water is used to transport minerals, sugars, and other substances to different parts of the plant. **Xylem tissue**, in the shape of a tube, transports water and minerals from the roots to different parts of the plant. Xylem also supports the stem. **Phloem tissue** transports glucose and nutrition from the site of photosynthesis to growing parts of the plant and storage. The xylem and phloem always lie adjacent to each other, and they are in the veins of a leaf (see drawing).

Do the following experiment to learn more about water in fruits and vegetables.

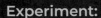
Compare Water Content of Fresh and Dried Fruit

Purpose: *To measure weight loss caused by dehydration.*

Materials

1 fresh apple

paring knife

cutting board

scale

baking sheet

vegetable oil cooking spray or parchment paper

1 fresh banana

½ cup orange juice

spatula

Procedure

1. Select fruit that is ripe, but not too ripe, and without blemishes. Wash the apples and towel dry.

2. Preheat the oven to 170 °F (75 °C).

3. Place an apple upright on a cutting board. Slice one side off the apple, staying about ½ inch away from the center of the apple so you miss the apple core and seeds. Slice off the three remaining sides. Place the sides of the apple on a scale and weigh (record in notebook).

4. Put each apple piece on its cut side and slice the apple into thin slices (as thin as possible).

5. Dip each apple slice in the orange juice to coat and shake off excess. (The vitamin C in the orange juice will help prevent the apple from turning brown due to enzymes.) Arrange the fruit in a single layer on a baking sheet sprayed with vegetable oil cooking spray or lined with parchment paper. Make sure the pieces do not touch each other.

6. Peel the banana and use the scale to weigh it (record weight in notebook). Next, slice into thin slices. Dip each slice into the orange juice to prevent browning and place on pan with apples.

7. Place pan in oven and allow room on each side of the pan so air circulates well and promotes even drying. After 90 minutes, lift each piece of fruit gently with a spatula and turn over.

8. The apples and bananas will need 5–6 hours to dry. If you have a convection oven, they will dry faster.

9. While the oven is on, open the oven door at least once an hour for a moment to allow air circulation and a chance for the moist air to leave the oven.

10. The fruit is ready when the slices are dry and leathery but may still be a *little* sticky to the touch.

11. Once cool, weigh the apples and record the weight. Also weigh the bananas and record the weight.

12. Leave dried fruit on sheet to cool overnight before placing in storage containers.

Observations

Record your answers to the following questions in your *Science Chef Notebook* (see "About This Book" for how to set up your own notebook).

1. How much did the apple weigh BEFORE it went in the oven?

   How much did the banana weigh BEFORE it went in the oven?

2. How much did the apple weigh AFTER it came out of the oven?

   How much did the banana weigh AFTER it came out of the oven?

3. Use this formula to calculate the weight loss for the *apple*.

   Weight Before Put in Oven – Weight After = Weight Loss

4. Use the formula again to calculate the weight loss for the *banana*.

5. Did the apples and/or bananas lose at least half of their original weight?

Dehydration of Fruit

Dehydration is the oldest method of preserving foods and was common long before there were supermarkets, refrigerators, and freezers. A fresh piece of fruit will eventually spoil, but dried fruit stays fresh a lot longer. Native Americans learned to dry fruits and vegetables (such as corn, squash, and apples) and even meat from deer and buffalo (which require additional steps). In the photo, you can compare the appearance of fresh and dried apples, fresh grapes and raisins, and fresh and dried bananas.

Apples

Grapes
Raisins

Bananas

What Happened in the Experiment?

Of course, the apple and banana slices lost weight after being baked in the oven at a very low temperature. Apples are 84% water and bananas are 74% water. Dried fruit will always retain about 20% of its water. As long as the apples and bananas were in the oven long enough, they both should have lost at least half of their original weight.

Overnight Slow-Cooked Maple Apple Oatmeal

Using a slow cooker to cook oatmeal overnight is the fastest way to have breakfast ready in the morning. Because the oats cook at a low temperature for a long period of time, this recipe calls for steel-cut oats, which need to be cooked longer than less processed oatmeal. Use a smaller size slow cooker for this dish so that the oatmeal doesn't dry out or brown at the edges (unless you want to double the recipe).

Difficulty: Beginner / **Time:** 20 minutes to prepare + overnight cooking (7–8 hours) / **Makes:** 4 servings

Ingredients

Vegetable oil cooking spray

½ cup dried apples

¼ cup raisins

¾ cup steel-cut oats (do not use old-fashioned or instant oats)

2¾ cups water

½ cup almond milk, soy milk, or other milk

½ teaspoon cinnamon

¼ cup maple syrup (optional)

Steps

1. Lightly spray the inside of the slow cooker with vegetable oil spray to prevent sticking.

2. With a cutting board and a paring knife, chop any large pieces of dried fruit (such as apples or apricots). Raisins or dried cranberries do not need to be cut.

3. In a bowl, lightly mix the dried fruit with the oats, water, milk, and cinnamon. Pour into slow cooker.

4. Cook on "Low" for 7–8 hours or until thick and creamy. Stir well before serving. Top with maple syrup, if desired.

5. Leftover oatmeal can be stored in the refrigerator and reheated in the microwave. Before microwaving, add a little water.

Variations

Banana Peanut Butter: Instead of dried apples, use dried bananas. Instead of maple syrup, use peanut butter.

Blueberry Almond: Instead of dried apples, use dried blueberries. Instead of maple syrup, use sliced almonds.

Cranberry Pecan: Instead of dried apples, used dried cranberries. Instead of maple syrup, use chopped pecans.

Apricot Brown Sugar Walnut: Instead of dried apples, use chopped dried apricots. Instead of maple syrup, use brown sugar. Add 1 tablespoon chopped walnuts to each serving.

If you use rolled or instant oats, the oatmeal will be overcooked and mushy.

Crunchy Granola

Granola is a baked cereal that combines grains with oil and sweeteners to bind the ingredients together. After baking, dried fruit, roasted nuts, and toasted seeds can be added.

Difficulty: Beginner / **Time:** 20 minutes to prepare, 30–40 minutes to cook, 20 minutes to cool / **Makes:** 9 ½-cup servings

Ingredients

1 cup raw pecans

½ cup raw almonds

(if using roasted nuts, add them to the granola with the dried cranberries after cooking)

4 cups old-fashioned oats (use only old-fashioned)

½ cup brown sugar

½ teaspoon salt

½ teaspoon cinnamon

¼ cup vegetable oil with neutral taste such as canola, corn, or soybean oils

¼ cup honey

1 teaspoon vanilla extract

¾ cup dried fruit (such as cranberries)

Steps

1. Preheat the oven to 300 °F (150 °C). Place parchment paper on a rectangular baking pan (about 13 inches × 18 inches) with sides to make cleanup easier.

2. If the nuts are large, use a paring knife and cutting board to cut them into a smaller size.

3. Mix the nuts (only if raw), oats, brown sugar, salt, and cinnamon in a large bowl.

4. In a saucepan, warm the oil and honey over medium heat. Stir in the vanilla extract.

5. Pour the oil and honey over the oats mixture.

6. Spread the oats mixture out onto a rectangular baking pan with sides. Your oats need to be a little crowded in the pan so they can stick together, but not so crowded that they don't cook evenly.

7. Bake at 300 °F (150 °C) for 30–40 minutes, stirring every 15 minutes.

8. Remove from the oven when lightly golden on top. Break up any clumps with a wooden spoon. Let cool for 20 minutes, then add the dried cranberries and roasted nuts (if you didn't use raw nuts).

9. When *completely* cooled (at least 1 hour), store in an airtight container where it should stay fresh for 7–10 days.

Use granola to top a yogurt parfait made with fresh, sliced fruit covered with ½ cup yogurt.

Bread Pudding with Raisins

Bread pudding is made by baking bread cubes in a milk and egg mixture. It is a great way to use up leftover bread. Traditional bread pudding also uses dried fruits such as raisins.

Difficulty: Intermediate / **Time:** 30 minutes to prepare and 45 minutes to bake / **Makes:** 8 servings

Ingredients

1 tablespoon butter to coat baking dish

6–7 thick slices of bread or ½ of brioche or challah bread (enough to make 6 cups bread cubes)

2 cups milk

3 tablespoons butter

2 eggs

⅓ cup sugar

1 teaspoon ground cinnamon

1 teaspoon vanilla extract

¼ teaspoon salt

½ cup raisins

whipped cream (optional)

Steps

1. Preheat the oven to 300°F (150°C).

2. Cut up the bread into 1-inch cubes. If the bread is fresh and needs to be dried out, place on a baking sheet and bake for about 4–8 minutes. You don't want to toast the bread, just dry it out.

3. After you remove the pan from the oven, set the oven to 350°F (175°C).

4. In a saucepan, heat the milk and butter over medium heat until the butter is melted and milk is getting hot. Set aside.

5. In a large bowl, beat the eggs. Then mix in the sugar, cinnamon, vanilla extract, and salt.

6. Stir the bread cubes and raisins into the egg mixture. Stir in milk mixture. Mix well so bread cubes are coated. Then pour into ungreased 9-inch × 13-inch baking pan or 9-inch round pan.

7. Bake at 350°F (175°C) for 40–45 minutes or until a knife inserted in several spots comes out clean. Remove from oven and let cool slightly before cutting.

8. Serve warm with whipped cream if desired. Refrigerate any leftover pudding.

Brioche is a rich, slightly sweet French bread that makes an outstanding bread pudding.

"No-Yeast" Holiday Stollen

Stollen is a traditional German fruitcake with a rich texture that is popular during December holidays. It is a colorful bread made with nuts, raisins, and other dried fruit.

Difficulty: Intermediate / **Time:** 50–60 minutes to prepare and 50 minutes to bake / **Makes:** 1 loaf of 15 slices

Ingredients

½ cup slivered almonds

1 cup all-purpose flour

1 cup whole wheat flour

½ cup sugar

1½ teaspoons baking powder

¼ teaspoon salt

6 tablespoons cold butter

1 cup ricotta cheese

1 large egg

1 egg yolk

1 teaspoon vanilla extract

½ teaspoon almond extract

½ cup candied fruits

⅔ cup raisins

1 tablespoon butter

1 tablespoon confectioner's sugar

Steps

1. Preheat the oven to 250 °F (120 °C). Place the almond slices on a cookie sheet and place into the oven. Lightly toast the almonds for approximately 5 minutes. You will smell the aroma of toasted nuts. Take them immediately out of the oven and let cool.

2. Change the temperature of the oven and preheat to 350 °F (175 °C).

3. In a large bowl, combine the flours, sugar, baking powder, and salt.

4. Using a pastry cutter with a rocking back-and-forth motion, cut the 6 tablespoons cold butter into the flour mixture until it resembles small peas. Make a well in the center of the ingredients.

5. In a small bowl, whisk together the ricotta cheese, eggs, vanilla extract, and almond extract. Fold in the almonds, candied fruits, and raisins.

6. Pour the ricotta mixture into the well of the flour mixture and mix the ingredients with a wooden spoon until well moistened.

7. Put some extra flour and the dough on a pastry or cutting board. Lightly knead the dough for about 5 minutes.

8. Roll out the dough into a large oval. Roll the dough into a loaf. Press in the edges to seal, forming a stollen shape.

9. Place the stollen on a cookie sheet lined with parchment paper.

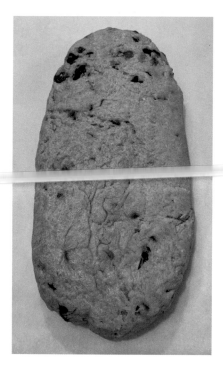

10. Bake the stollen at 350 °F (175 °C) for 45–50 minutes or until golden brown. Remove from oven.

11. Melt 1 tablespoon butter in the microwave. Brush the butter on the stollen with a pastry brush. After 5 minutes, dust liberally with confectioner's sugar.

12. Transfer the stollen to a cooling rack and allow to cool thoroughly.

Candied fruits are made by soaking whole or cut fruit in a sugar syrup for days at a time so the sugar penetrates into the cells of the fruit.

Video at http:// www.wiley .com/go/ sciencechef.

Nutrient Content of Recipes

Note: Optional ingredients and garnishes are not included in the calculations.

Nutrient calculations are for the standard recipe, not the variations.

Nutrient analysis completed by Wendy Hess, MS, RD, Consulting in Nutrition Analysis, Burlington, Vermont.

Recipe and Serving Size	Calories	Carbohydrate (grams)	Added Sugars (grams)	Fiber (grams)	Fat (grams)	Saturated Fat (grams)	Protein (grams)
Chapter 1							
Basic Baked Potatoes – 1 potato	134	27	0	3	1	1	4
Broccoli and Cheddar Stuffed Potatoes – 1 potato	309	35	0	5	13	7	15
Smashed Potatoes – ½ cup	125	17	0	1	6	2	2
Air-Fried French Fries – ¼ recipe	153	21	0	2	7	1	2
Potato Skins with Cheddar and Salsa – 4 skins	320	55	0	10	7	4	10
Crunchy Country Potato Salad – ⅛ recipe	110	23	0	2	2	0	3
Create-a-Potato Party – 1 potato (plain)	84	19	0	1	0	0	2
Quinoa-and Salsa-Stuffed Sweet Potatoes with Awesome Avocado Sauce – 1 potato	569	95	0	9	17	2	13

(Continued)

Recipe and Serving Size	Calories	Carbohy-drate (grams)	Added Sugars (grams)	Fiber (grams)	Fat (grams)	Saturated Fat (grams)	Protein (grams)
Chapter 2							
The Best Popcorn – 2 cups	116	13	0	3	6	1	2
"New" Fashioned Kettle Corn – 2 cups	236	23	10	3	15	7	2
Popcorn Power Bars – 1 square	163	23	12	1	7	3	2
Trail Mix Popcorn – 1 cup	143	22	1	3	5	1	3
"Movie Time" Cheddar Cheese and Chive Popcorn – 2 cups	230	14	0	3	17	8	4
Popcorn Santa Fe – 1 square	119	12	0	1	7	3	3
Springtime Pastel Popcorn Treats – 1 popcorn ball	289	44	26	3	12	7	2
Chapter 3							
"A Plus" Air-Fried Onion Rings – ¼ recipe	251	44	0	1	4	1	10
Cheesy Cauliflower and Onion Bake – ⅛ recipe	160	12	0	2	11	5	6
Chapter 4							
Awesome Avocado Toast – 1 recipe	403	31	0	16	31	5	8
High Tea Cinnamon Toast – 2 slices	308	49	25	5	10	5	7
Peanut Butter and Jelly French Toast Cutouts – 1 sandwich	377	53	9	5	13	3	15
Linzer Tart French Toast – 1 sandwich	279	47	7	4	5	1	12
Strawberry Butter – 2 tablespoons	148	3	2	0	15	10	0

Recipe and Serving Size	Calories	Carbohydrate (grams)	Added Sugars (grams)	Fiber (grams)	Fat (grams)	Saturated Fat (grams)	Protein (grams)
Creamy Herb and Chive Spread – 2 tablespoons	73	2	0	0	7	4	1
Ralph's Zippy Hummus – 2 tablespoons	107	7	0	2	8	1	3
Chapter 5							
Southwestern Dinner Salad – 1 salad (¼ recipe)	302	41	2	14	12	2	11
"Aquafabulous" Cornbread – 1 square	131	23	8	1	4	1	2
Santa Fe Cheesy Black Bean Soup – 1 cup	207	30	0	11	5	2	12
Quick-and-Easy Lunchtime Burrito – 1 burrito	526	53	0	1	23	9	28
Chapter 6							
Over-the-Rainbow Mac and Cheese – ⅛ recipe	334	36	0	2	14	8	14
Chile Con Queso Dip – ¼ cup	175	13	0	1	11	5	6
Chapter 7							
All-American White Bread – 1 slice	120	21	2	1	2	1	4
Basic Pizza Dough – 1 recipe	1,645	293	4	12	32	5	42
Possibilities Pizza – 1 slice	341	47	1	3	12	4	12
"Saucy" Sausage and Veggie Stromboli – 1 slice	357	41	1	2	16	4	13
Monkey Bread – 1/15 serving	315	54	22	1	9	3	6

(Continued)

Recipe and Serving Size	Calories	Carbohydrate (grams)	Added Sugars (grams)	Fiber (grams)	Fat (grams)	Saturated Fat (grams)	Protein (grams)
Chapter 8							
Baking Powder Drop Biscuits – 1 biscuit	133	17	0	1	6	4	3
Breakfast Strawberry Shortcakes – 1 shortcake	156	23	4	1	6	4	3
Picnic Time Carrot, Coconut, and Currant Bread – 1 slice	221	28	10	3	12	2	3
Protein-Packed Blueberry Pancakes – 1 pancake	174	24	1	2	7	1	6
Basic Muffins with Variations – 1 basic muffin	175	26	8	1	6	1	4
Chapter 9							
The Best Veggie Quiche Recipe – 1 slice	285	17	1	1	19	9	11
Custom Omelets – 1 plain omelet	167	2	0	0	11	4	13
Angel Food Cake – 1 slice	119	24	15	0	0	0	5
Chapter 10							
Trendy Tuna Salad – 1 scoop, ¼ recipe	88	5	0	1	2	0	14
Italian Dressing – 1 tablespoon	66	1	0	0	7	1	0
Rich Raspberry Dressing – 1 tablespoon	33	2	0	0	3	0	0
Layered Lunch-time Salads in a Jar – 1 salad	219	23	4	4	13	2	3

Recipe and Serving Size	Calories	Carbohy-drate (grams)	Added Sugars (grams)	Fiber (grams)	Fat (grams)	Saturated Fat (grams)	Protein (grams)
Default Delicious Three Bean Salad – ⅛ recipe	132	19	0	5	4	1	6
Paninis with Mayo Pesto Dressing – 1 sandwich	744	36	0	3	61	16	16
Fresh Fruit Cocktail with Honey Yogurt Dressing – ¼ recipe	193	44	8	4	1	1	5
Chapter 11							
Garden Fresh Tomato Sauce – ½ cup	23	5	0	1	1	0	1
Creamy Blender Pesto Sauce – ½ cup	216	2	0	0	23	3	2
Roasted Red Pepper Pesto Sauce with Artichokes, Olives, and Tomatoes – ¼ recipe	316	45	0	8	10	1	11
Chapter 12							
Aunt Teresa's Old-Fashioned Bread-and-Butter Pickles – ¼ cucumber	34	8	5	0	0	0	0
Cool Crunchy Refrigerator Pickles – ¼ cucumber	25	6	2	0	0	0	0
Chapter 13							
Vita-Packed Tri Berry Smoothie – 1 serving (about 1 cup)	144	34	8	4	1	0	4
"Tropicalicious" Island Mango Smoothie – 1 serving (about 1 cup)	246	58	8	6	1	1	5

(Continued)

Recipe and Serving Size	Calories	Carbohy-drate (grams)	Added Sugars (grams)	Fiber (grams)	Fat (grams)	Saturated Fat (grams)	Protein (grams)
Green-n-Lean Warrior Smoothie – 1 serving (about 1 cup)	194	46	8	6	2	0	3
Chapter 14							
Fruity Popsicles – 1 popsicle	41	10	0	0	0	0	0
Yogurt-Fruit Swirl Popsicles – 1 popsicle	51	8	0	1	1	1	3
Pudding Popsicles – 1 popsicle	100	19	15	0	1	1	3
Chapter 15							
Power Cookie Mix – 1 cup mix	641	75	4	2	32	20	13
Peanut Butter Cookie Treats – 1 cookie	94	13	8	0	4	2	2
M&M Cookies – 1 cookie	111	15	9	0	5	3	2
Major Molasses Cookie Bites – 1 cookie	86	14	8	0	3	2	1
Delicious Double Chocolate Honey Brownies – 1 brownie	174	24	17	2	9	5	2
Chapter 16							
Homemade Honey-Roasted Peanut Butter – 1 oz (about 1½ tablespoons)	178	7	1	2	15	2	7
The Best Banana Almond Milkshake – 1 cup	113	16	6	1	5	2	2
"Peanutty" Coco-Chocolate Energy Treats – 2 treats	178	25	9	2	7	2	4

Recipe and Serving Size	Calories	Carbohydrate (grams)	Added Sugars (grams)	Fiber (grams)	Fat (grams)	Saturated Fat (grams)	Protein (grams)
Easy Cashew Fettuccini with Sun-Dried Tomatoes and Chives – 1 serving (¼ recipe)	607	76	0	8	24	5	23
Chapter 17							
Jammin' Red Raspberry Jam – ~~tablespoons~~	104	26	20	3	0	0	0
Whole-Wheat Snickerdoodle Surprise Muffins – 1 each	186	28	8	2	7	1	3
Chicken Breasts Glazed with Peach Jam – 1 chicken breast half	327	39	30	0	6	1	27
Chapter 18							
Overnight Slow-Cooked Maple Apple Oatmeal – ¼ serving	178	35	0	5	3	0	4
Crunchy Granola – ½ cup serving	445	59	24	7	21	2	8
Bread Pudding with Raisins – ⅛ recipe	237	32	8	1	10	5	6
"No Yeast" Holiday Stollen – 1 slice	241	33	11	2	10	5	5

Glossary

added sugars Sweeteners added to foods and beverages for flavor.

amino acids The components (building blocks) of **protein**.

aquafaba The liquid found in a can of chickpeas.

bacteria Microscopic single-celled organisms that can be found everywhere. Most not harmful but some can cause serious health in

baking powder A mixture of a weak acid and a base used in baking to increase the volume of baked goods and give them a tender texture. In the presence of moisture or heat, the acid reacts with the base to produce carbon dioxide bubbles.

beans Seeds found in a special group of flowering plants. Examples include pinto beans and dark red kidney beans.

beat To move the utensil back and forth to blend ingredients together.

boil To be at the boiling point – 212 °F for water. When a liquid boils, that means it is turning into steam (the gaseous state of water).

calorie A measure of the energy in food.

carbohydrate A group of nutrients that include sugar, starch, and fiber.

cell wall A structure found around each plant cell that protects and supports the cell.

chop To cut into irregularly sized pieces.

colloid Heterogenous mixture in which the dispersed particles are bigger than those found in solutions.

conduction A method of heat transfer in which heat moves from something that is hot to something touching it (such as from a hot frying pan to eggs in the pan).

convection A method of heat transfer in which heat spreads by the movement of hot air, such as hot air in an oven, or the movement of hot liquid, such as in a pot of boiling water.

cream To mix a solid fat (usually butter) with sugar by pressing them against the bowl with the back of a spoon until they look creamy.

crystal A clear, solid substance that has smooth surfaces and is balanced in shape on all sides.

custard A smooth semisolid gel created when eggs and milk cook together.

dehydration Loss or removal of water.

denaturation When proteins lose their special shape and unfold/untwist. Caused by whipping, heat, and acid. Results in proteins that cannot perform their normal functions.

dice To cut into cubes of the same size.

embryo The part of a seed that develops into a new plant, including the roots, leaves, and stem.

emulsion A stable mixture of two liquids that would normally separate from each other.

enzyme Proteins present in human cells and cells of fruits and vegetables. Primary job is to speed up chemical reactions in the cells.

fat A nutrient that supplies more energy than any other nutrient.

fermentation A process in which small organisms (bacteria, yeast) convert complex molecules into simpler ones, such as when yeast feed on sugars in bread dough and make carbon dioxide gas.

fiber A variety of substances present in plant foods that can't be digested in the intestines. A health-promoting nutrient.

fold To mix ingredients using a gentle over-and-under motion with a utensil.

foodborne illness A disease caused by substances in food, such as bacteria and molds, that cause symptoms such as nausea, vomiting, and diarrhea.

food science A scientific discipline that seeks to understand how foods cook and also how foods can be processed and preserved so everyone has access to safe, nutritious food.

freezing point The temperature at which a liquid turns into a solid.

fructose A natural sugar found in ripe fruits.

fruits Part of a plant that contains seeds to grow new plants.

gas A phase of matter with no fixed shape. Gas will take both the shape and volume of the container it is in.

gel A special type of colloid that is liquid but behaves like a solid. At high temperatures, a gel is liquid, but at colder temperatures, a gel is solid. A jam is an example of a gel.

gelatinization When heated in liquid, starch granules absorb water and swell, making the liquid thicken.

germination - See **sprouting**.

glucose A natural sugar that is the main source of energy for the body and in plants.

gluten An elastic protein in flour that allows bread dough to expand or rise without bursting. Formed when flour and water combine.

grate To rub a food across a grater's tiny punched holes to produce small or fine pieces of food.

herbs The stem or leafy parts of certain plants that grow in temperate climates used to season and flavor foods.

heterogeneous mixture A type of mixture where the substances are not well mixed or evenly distributed.

highly processed foods Mass-produced packaged foods often high in sugars and/or bad fats such as cookies, candy, ice cream, sweetened breakfast cereals, many crackers and chips, luncheon meats, and many canned foods.

homogeneous mixture A mixture in which all the substances are evenly distributed throughout—such as salt in water.

hypothesis A proposed explanation (educated guess) that will be tested through experimentation and study.

kneading To work dough (usually bread dough) into a smooth mass by pressing and folding. Helps incorporate air, distribute ingredients, and develop gluten, which lets bread dough rise and expand.

leaves Part of a plant that uses sunlight, carbon dioxide, and water to make food and also oxygen.

liquids A phase of matter that appears between the solid and gas phases. A liquid will take the shape of its container.

Maillard reaction A browning of food when exposed to heat that creates new flavors and aromas. The browning is due to a chemical reaction between protein and sugar in the presence of heat and dryness.

mince To chop very fine.

mix To combine ingredients so that they are all evenly distributed.

mixture A combination of substances that do not react chemically with each other, such as sand in water or the ingredients in a soft drink. Mixtures can be solids, liquids, or gases.

molecule Two or more atoms that form a substance with properties different from those of the atoms of which it is made.

natural sugar A sugar, such as glucose or fructose, that occurs naturally in foods.

nutrient The nourishing substances in foods that give you energy, allow your body to grow, and keep you healthy.

nutrition A science that looks at the calories and nutrients in food and beverages and how they affect your body and health.

oil Fats that are liquid at room temperature.

pectin A substance found in many plants that gives physical strength to cell walls. Used to thicken jams and jellies.

pesto An Italian sauce with ingredients such as olive oil and basil leaves, which give it its distinctive green color.

phase change A change from one state (solid, liquid, or gas) to another without a change in chemical composition.

phase of matter The states in which matter can exist. Three common states are solid, liquid, and gas. There are other phases of matter such as plasma.

phloem tissue The part of a plant that transports glucose and nutrition from the site of photosynthesis to growing parts of the plant and storage.

photosynthesis A process in which green plants use sunlight, water, and carbon dioxide to make carbohydrates (such as glucose) and oxygen.

pizza stone A cooking surface usually made of ceramic or stone that is heated in the oven before pizza is placed on it. Cooks pizza more evenly and allows the crust to get crisp.

pod A protected structure that hangs down from the bean plant and contains beans.

pollen A powdery yellowish grain made by flowering plants that must be transferred between parts of the flower in order for the flower to produce a seed.

pollination When pollen is transferred between parts of a plant or tree's flower (often by bees), which then allows the flower to produce a seed.

precipitate A solid that comes out of a supersaturated solution.

protein A nutrient present in all body cells that is needed for growth and health.

purée To change a solid food into a thick liquid.

quick breads Breads, like muffins and pancakes, that use baking powder (not yeast) to rise during baking.

radiation A method of heat transfer when heat is transferred by waves as in sunlight or the glowing coals of a charcoal grill. Microwave ovens also transmit radiation waves.

ramekin A ceramic dish that holds individual servings of food, such as macaroni and cheese, to be cooked in the oven.

reproductive stage A stage of growth characterized by the plant being able to reproduce through flowers which contain seeds.

roots Main part of a plant that is underground and absorbs water and nutrients from the soil. Also helps keep the plant firmly anchored to the ground.

roux A thickener used by chefs that is made of flour and fat cooked together.

saturated solution A solution that contains the maximum concentration of a solute.

sauté To cook quickly in a pan over medium-high heat in a small amount of fat.

scientific method A method to seek new knowledge that involves identifying a question and hypothesizing its answer, and then gathering and analyzing data to see if the hypothesis is supported.

seed Part of a flowering plant that, once put in the ground, will grow into a new plant.

seed coat A protective covering of a seed.

seedling A young plant that grows from a seed and continues to develop its roots and leaves.

shred To rub a food across a surface with medium to large holes or slits to produce small pieces of food.

simmer To cook in a liquid that is just below boiling.

slice To cut into uniform slices.

solid A phase of matter. A solid holds its shape.

solution A special type of homogenous mixture in which a substance, called the solute, dissolves in the solvent (which is frequently water). The solute is evenly distributed in the solvent.

spices The dried seeds, fruits, barks, or roots of certain plants that are used to season and flavor foods.

sprouting (also called **germination**) When a seed pushes roots into the soil and a stem with leaves pushes up through the soil into the sunlight.

steam Water in the gas phase, which is formed when water boils.

stem Part of a plant that supports the plant and carries water and nutrients to the leaves.

suspension Heterogenous mixture in which the solute particles do not dissolve in the solvent but instead are suspended temporarily and will eventually separate and settle.

vegetative stage The period of growth for a plant between germination and flowering (reproductive stage).

viscosity Resistance of a fluid to flow.

whip To beat rapidly using a circular motion, usually with a wire whip, to incorporate air into the mixture (such as in making whipped cream).

whisk To beat ingredients together with a wire whip until they are well blended.

whole foods Foods that are not processed or minimally processed and do not have added ingredients such as sugar.

xylem tissue A tube-like shape that transports water and minerals from the roots of a plant to other plant parts.

yeast A tiny, single-celled organism that makes bread dough rise because it produces carbon dioxide gas when it eats sugars.

Index